SAVING MONEY AND LIVING WELL
Secret to Help You Live An Enjoyable Life While Living Well

Adam L. Rogers

Copyright © 2024 by Adam L. Rogers
All rights reserved.
No part of this publication may be reproduced, distributed, or transmitted in any form or by any means, including photocopying, recording, or other electronic or mechanical methods, without the prior written permission of the author, except in the case of brief quotations embodied in critical reviews and certain other noncommercial uses permitted by copyright law.

About the author

American financial expert Adam L. Rogers has over ten years of expertise as a trustworthy business adviser. He has a wide range of expertise in personal finance, budgeting, and strategic financial planning. Adam is committed to simplifying complex financial concepts so that everyone can achieve financial security.

Table of contents

INTRODUCTION
    WOULD YOU RATHER BE SEXY OR RICH
CHAPTER ONE
    THE GOOD LIFE IS NOT WHAT WE THINK IT IS
CHAPTER 2
    WRITTEN GOAL CAN CHANGE YOUR LIFE
CHAPTER 3
    WE GET MORE WHEN WE GIVE
CHAPTER 4
    GIVE EVERY DOLLAR A JOB
CHAPTER 5
    AGE YOUR MONEY
CHAPTER 6
    TEACHING YOUR KIDS TO BUDGET
CHAPTER 7
    GET READY TO INVEST
CHAPTER 8
    INVESTMENT ISN'T ONLY FOR RICH PEOPLE
CHAPTER 9
    SAVE WHILE SLEEPING

INTRODUCTION
WOULD YOU RATHER BE SEXY OR RICH

The idea that we must first organize every aspect of our personal finances before we can begin managing our money paralyzes far too many of us.

How hard is it to make a grilled cheese sandwich without becoming an Iron Chef? No, because cooking the next most difficult dish will be simpler after you've prepared your first one. Being the most intelligent person in the room is not the most significant component in becoming wealthy; starting is.

One person is primarily to blame for your financial issues: YOU. You should put more effort into changing the things that you can control about your financial condition rather than blaming "the economy" and corporate America. Similar to how the diet industry has overloaded us with options, personal finance is a bewildering jumble of exaggerated claims, misconceptions, and outright lies. However, we can only hold businesses and the media accountable for our failure to take personal responsibility and step up, learn this information, and get going while we have access to food and money. As a result, a large number of us become obese, materialistic, and impoverished.

Had any of the people who were criticizing the government, CEOs, and bad banks even read a single book on finance? And yet they thought they would succeed financially?

Instead of just saying, "I guess that's how much I spent last month," what if you could actively choose how you spend your money? What if you could create an automated savings system and make all of your accounts operate together? What if you could invest fearlessly and simply on a regular basis? What do you think? Yes, you can!

Do you truly want to be wealthy when you claim you do? Or are you merely looking to appear wealthy? Do you wish to get wealthy? Or are you simply looking to spend it?

This book asks you to defy conventional wisdom at every turn. It means putting less emphasis on social currency and more on measurable outcomes.

It is our nature to be amiable. to blend in with our community, culture, and tribe. Thus, we frequently adopt their viewpoints. However, by definition, an outlier or oddity doesn't belong.

CHAPTER ONE
THE GOOD LIFE IS NOT WHAT WE THINK IT IS

"The good life"—what is it? Among the first philosophical queries is this one. Different questions have been raised on how one should live. But these are essentially just questions about what it means to "live well." Everyone wants to have a good life, after all, and nobody desires "the bad life."

However, the question is more complicated than it seems. Philosophers are experts at revealing hidden complexity, and one idea that requires much unpacking is the ideal life.

The Righteous Life

The term "good" is mostly used to convey moral acceptance. Therefore, we may simply mean that someone is a good person—someone who is brave, honest, trustworthy, kind, selfless, generous, helpful, loyal, principled, and so on—when we say that they are living well or have lived a good life.

Many of the most significant virtues are possessed and exercised by them. Additionally, they don't live their lives just for their personal enjoyment; instead, they dedicate a portion of their time to endeavors that better society, whether it is via their employment, their involvement in volunteer work, or their interactions with family and friends.

This ethical idea of what constitutes a good life has many supporters. Both Socrates and Plato ranked virtue as the highest good above all other purportedly beneficial things, including pleasure, prosperity, or power.

Socrates pushes this idea too far in Plato's Gorgias dialogue. He contends that a virtuous guy who has his eyes gouged out and is tortured to death is more fortunate than a corrupt person who has exploited wealth and power dishonorably, and that it is far better to suffer injustice than to do it.

Plato elaborates on this point in more depth in his magnum opus, The Republic. He says that the morally upright person has a kind of inner harmony, whereas the wicked person, regardless of wealth, power, or pleasure, is disharmonious and fundamentally at war with both the world and himself.

However, it should be noted that Plato supports his claims in the Gorgias and the Republic with a fantastical description of a hereafter where good people receive rewards and bad people receive punishment.

A life lived in accordance with God's laws is considered the good life in many religions as well. Living this way—keeping the rules and following the ceremonies—makes one pious. And such piety will be honored in most religions. It goes without saying that a lot of people in this life do not get their due.

However, devoted believers are sure that their devotion won't go in vain. The Christian martyrs knew they would soon be in heaven, therefore they sang as they died. Hindus believe that their good intents and deeds will be rewarded by the law of karma, while their evil deeds and desires will be punished, either in this incarnation or in subsequent ones.

The Life of Enjoyment
One of the first people to firmly assert that the ability to enjoy life is what makes it worthwhile to live was the ancient Greek philosopher Epicurus. Fun, enjoyable, and, well, nice are the qualities of pleasure! Hedonism is the belief that pleasure is the

ultimate good, or, to put it another way, that pleasure is the reason life is worthwhile.

When used to describe an individual, the term "hedonist" carries a slightly negative meaning. It implies that they are committed to what some have referred to as the "lower" pleasures—food, alcohol, sex, and general sensual indulgence.

Some of Epicurus's contemporaries believed he was promoting and living this kind of lifestyle, and even in modern times, someone who is particularly appreciative of food and drink is referred to as a "epicure." However, this is an inaccurate portrayal of Epicureanism. Without a doubt, Epicurus extolled a variety of joys. However, he disapproved of our losing ourselves in sensuous revelry for a number of reasons:

- Since overindulgence tends to limit our variety of joys and produce health problems, doing so will likely decrease our pleasures over time.
- "Higher" joys like companionship and education are just as significant as "pleasures of the flesh."
- A good life must be morally upright. Epicurus agreed with Plato on this point,

even though they couldn't agree on the importance of pleasure.

This hedonistic idea of the ideal life is arguably still prevalent in Western culture today. Even in casual conversation, when we say someone is "living the good life," we most often mean that they are indulging in a wide range of leisure activities, such as skiing, scuba diving, fine dining, nice wine, and sunbathing by the pool with a lovely companion.

This hedonistic idea of the good life is centered on subjective sensations, which is crucial. According to this perspective, a person is said to be "happy" when they "feel good," and a happy life is one that is full of numerous "feel good" events.

The Happy Life

While Epicurus prioritizes pleasure and Socrates emphasizes virtue, Aristotle, another renowned Greek philosopher, approaches the question of what makes for a happy life from a wider perspective. According to Aristotle, everyone aspires to happiness.

Many things are only valuable to us in the service of other goals. We value money, for instance, because it enables us to buy the things we want, and we value leisure because it gives us the opportunity to spend time doing the activities we enjoy. But rather than viewing happiness as a means to an end, we appreciate it for its own sake. It has intrinsic value instead of being valued as an instrument.

Consequently, Aristotle defined happiness as the ideal life. But what exactly does that mean? Nowadays, a lot of people instantly connect subjectivism with happiness: As per their perspective, an individual's life is considered happy when they are generally content and have a positive mental state.

But when it comes to happiness, there's a problem with this logic. Imagine a powerful sadist who spends a lot of time gratifying his disgusting desires. Imagine a couch potato who does nothing but sit around playing video games and binge-watch old TV shows while using cannabis and drinking beer. These individuals may have a great deal of enjoyable subjective experiences. Can we, however, really claim that they are "living well"?

Aristotle would undoubtedly answer no. He agrees with Socrates that living a decent life requires moral greatness. Moreover, he agrees with Epicurus that a fulfilling life will comprise a variety of delightful experiences. We cannot genuinely say that someone is living a nice life if they are always in pain or are dissatisfied on a regular basis.

But when defining what it is to live properly, Aristotle takes an objectivist approach rather than a subjectivist one. Though internal emotions have a significant role, they are not the sole one. A few objective requirements must also be fulfilled.

As an illustration:
- Virtue: They must be morally virtue-possessed.
- Health: They should have good health and live a respectably long life.
- Prosperity: They should be well-off (by Aristotle's standards, this meant having enough money to not need to work at a job they wouldn't choose to do).
- Friendship: They must have strong ties. Aristotle thought that as people are social beings by nature, leading a misanthropic, hermit, or solitary life could hardly be regarded as the ideal way to live.
- Respect: People should show them respect in return. Glory and renown are not necessary in Aristotle's view; in fact, he thinks that pursuing fame can be just as bad in terms of

misguiding others as pursuing excessive wealth. Still, it is best when other people acknowledge a person's qualities and achievements.
- What they need is good fortune. This illustrates Aristotle's common sense. Disaster or loss can sadly interrupt anyone's life.
- Engagement: They must make use of what makes them uniquely human. This is the reason why couch potatoes are not enjoying satisfying lives, even though they profess to be content. Aristotle believed that human reason is what distinguishes humans from other animals. Therefore, the good life is characterized as a state in which a person cultivates and applies their logical faculties through pursuits such as scientific investigation, philosophical discussion, artistic creation, or legislative action. He most likely would have added some technological development if he were still with us today.

If, when the time comes to pass away, you can confidently check off all these boxes, you have lived a good life and achieved the good life. Of course, the majority of individuals in the modern world do not belong to Aristotle's leisure class. They require employment to survive.

Nevertheless, we continue to think that, in any case, the ideal scenario is to be making a living doing what you enjoy. As a result, it is frequently seen as a huge blessing for individuals who are able to pursue their career.

The Life That Is Meaningful

According to recent studies, having children does not always translate into happiness compared to not having children. Indeed, parents tend to experience higher levels of stress and lower levels of satisfaction during the years they spend raising children, particularly once they have grown into teenagers. Nonetheless, having kids seems to give people a greater sense of purpose in life, even though it may not necessarily make them happier.

The primary source of meaning in life for a lot of people is their family's well-being, particularly that of their children and grandkids. This perspective has a very lengthy history. Having several self-sufficient children was considered a sign of good fortune in the past.

Of course, a person's life might have value from other sources as well. For example, someone might devote themselves entirely to a certain type of activity, such as scholarly labor, artistic creation, or scientific study. They might dedicate their lives to a cause, such as the preservation of the environment or the battle against prejudice. Alternatively, they might be fully involved in and absorbed in a specific community, like a school, a sports team, or a church.

The Complete Existence

A proverb among the Greeks read, "Call no man happy until he is dead." This is a wise move. You could even want to change it to: Don't call a man joyful till he's dead. Because occasionally someone can seem to have a wonderful life and be able to check all the boxes—virtue, prosperity, companionship, respect, meaning, etc.—only to later turn out to be someone else entirely.

An excellent illustration of this is Jimmy Saville, the British TV personality who was well liked during his lifetime but was revealed to be a serial sexual predator after his death.

Situations such as these highlight the significant benefit of adopting an objectivist definition of well-being over a subjectivist one. Maybe Jimmy Saville had a good time in his life. Of course, we wouldn't want to claim that he had a perfect life. A truly good life is one that fulfills all or most of the above-mentioned criteria for admirability and envy.

What gives life meaning
The Covid era has set additional constraints on many people's ability to construct the kind of lives they want, making it difficult to think about what it means to live a decent life. In light of lockdowns, someone who values socializing with friends has probably had less opportunity to do so; someone who enjoys traveling has presumably taken significantly fewer trips than in past years. Which orientation—against meaning, happiness, or psychological richness—might be most helpful at this time?

According to Westgate, each individual would naturally have a different response, but for those who have been at the forefront of the pandemic—such as vital workers and healthcare providers—"focusing on meaning and psychological richness might be more salient." In addition to experiencing difficult, dramatic occasions that are linked to psychological richness, their work is genuinely important.

If you're among those who don't think your life is going well right now, considering the various aspects of a fulfilling, meaningful, and psychologically rich existence may help you identify the adjustments you want to make.

In addition, the authors of the research point out that there might be even more aspects that they haven't taken into consideration if you believe that your life is wonderful right now but don't fit into any of the three categories they outline. These might include an intellectual life, a creative life, or a loving, caring life.

A fascinating and diverse existence
What does a life rich in psychology entail? It is characterized by "interesting experiences in which novelty and/or complexity are accompanied by profound changes in perspective," according to authors Erin Westgate, an assistant professor of psychology at the University of Florida, and Shige Oishi, a professor of psychology at the University of Virginia.

One method that college students frequently add psychological richness to their lives is through studying abroad. They are frequently forced to reevaluate the social mores of their own civilizations when they get more knowledge about the history and customs of a foreign nation. Making the decision to pursue a challenging new job path or becoming fully immersed in avant-garde work (the paper specifically mentions James Joyce's Ulysses) might also give one the impression that their life is more psychologically rich.

Importantly, an event need not be enjoyable to be considered mentally enhancing. It may even prove to be difficult. Even though it may be difficult to feel as though you're leading a particularly happy or purposeful life after experiencing a natural disaster or war, you can still develop psychologically from the experience. Alternatively, you may experience less spectacular but no less terrible circumstances, such as chronic sickness, unemployment, or infertility. You may suffer, whatever the details, but you will still benefit from the way your experience changes the way you see the world and yourself.

According to Westgate, it's critical to include psychological complexity in our ideas of what a successful life can entail since it "makes room for challenge and difficulty." It goes beyond simply noting that "everything goes well and smoothly."

Stretching oneself and enduring painful situations have benefits.

On the other hand, she argues that if we limit our expectations of what a good life is, we could come to the "incredibly presumptive and dismissive of people's experiences and values" conclusion that someone whose life is neither hedonic nor eudaimonic must consequently have a bad existence.

Who desires depth in psychology?
There is no right or wrong way to live a hedonic, eudaimonic, or psychologically rich life. According to Westgate, "someone whose life is good, it tends to be good in many ways, not just in one." It is possible that your life is happy, meaningful, and full with life-changing events. How fortunate you are!

However, people might also decide to give one way of life a higher priority than another. The Big Five personality traits, for instance, were examined in the study amongst individuals of various nations. Conscientiousness, openness to experience, neuroticism, extraversion, and agreeableness are the five personality traits that are measured by the Big

Five test, which is thought to be the most scientific of personality tests.

The study found that those with high "openness to experience" scores had higher odds of leading psychologically fulfilling lives. According to Oishi and Westgate, "vivid fantasy, artistic sensitivity, depth of feeling, behavioral flexibility, intellectual curiosity, and unconventional attitudes" are generally indicative of an openness to experience.

It makes sense, then, that someone who is often creative and outspoken would be driven to a life of constant change. As the writers point out, "A meaningful life or a happy life do not fully reflect the spectrum of human motivation for these and other important reasons." Repeated and boring lives can also be happy and fulfilling.

Does psychological richness occur in a WEIRD way?

According to the study, those who pursued meaningful lives were fairly evenly divided among the Big Five qualities, with extraversion, conscientiousness, and low neuroticism being the traits most closely related with happy lives. It's interesting to note that the authors also discovered that individuals who lead psychologically rich lives were more likely to support social change and be politically liberal, whilst individuals who lead happy or fulfilling lives were more likely to favor maintaining the status quo.

Whether the pursuit of a psychologically full life is unique to WEIRD (Western, educated, industrialized, affluent, and democratic) nations or something that only a privileged individual with their other needs supplied would want was one of the writers' main concerns. However, the study discovered that the notion of a psychologically rich life wasn't more prevalent in wealthy or Western nations than it wasn't. Furthermore, although happy persons were more likely to be of a higher socioeconomic class, the authors found no evidence of a substantial correlation between income and meaningful and psychologically rich lives.

CHAPTER 2
WRITTEN GOAL CAN CHANGE YOUR LIFE

A lot of people experience a sense of being lost in the world. They put up a lot of effort, but it doesn't appear to be paying off.

They haven't given their lives much thought or established any official goals, which is one of the main reasons they feel this way. Would you, after all, embark on a significant voyage without having a clear notion of where you were going? Most likely not!

How to Make a Goal

Think about what you want to accomplish first, then make a commitment to it. Set SMART (specific, measurable, attainable, relevant, and time-bound) goals that motivate you and put them in paper to make them feel more genuine. Next, make a list of the steps you need to do to achieve your objective and mark them off as you complete them.

Setting objectives helps you stay focused on your ideal future and motivates you to bring it to pass.

The goal-setting process aids in determining your life's direction. Having a clear goal in mind makes it easier to direct your efforts in the appropriate directions. Additionally, you'll be able to identify distractions that could easily mislead you with ease.

Why make goals?
Athletes at the highest levels, prosperous businesspeople, and achievers in every endeavor have objectives. Establishing objectives provides you with both immediate and long-term drive. It helps you make the most of your life by focusing your knowledge acquisition and assisting with time and resource management.

Setting specific, measurable goals can help you quantify your progress and feel proud of yourself when you reach them. This will help you make progress in a task that may have previously seemed like an endless, futile slog. As you become more aware of your own proficiency and capacity to accomplish the objectives you have set for yourself, you will also gain more self-confidence.

Getting Started with Setting Personal Objectives
You establish your objectives on several levels:

In order to attain your large-scale goals, you must first establish your "big picture" of what you want to do with your life (or over, say, the next ten years).

You then divide these into the increasingly smaller benchmarks that you need to meet in order to fulfill your lifelong ambitions.

After you have your plan in place, you can finally work on it to accomplish these objectives.

For this reason, we look at your lifetime goals at the beginning of the goal-setting process. We next narrow it down to the things you can do today to begin working toward goals, then next year, next month, next week, and so on, for example, the next five years.

Step1: Make lifelong objectives

Thinking on what you want to accomplish in your lifetime—or at least, by a meaningful and distant age in the future—is the first step towards creating personal objectives. Establishing lifelong objectives provides you with the broad viewpoint that influences all other areas of your decision-making.

Try to create goals in some of the following areas (or in other categories where they are relevant to you) to provide a wide, balanced coverage of all significant areas in your life:

- Career: What goals do you have for yourself, or what level do you wish to achieve?
- Financial: What is your desired income and by when? Regarding your career ambitions, how does this relate?
- Education: Are there any specific topics you'd like to learn more about? What knowledge and abilities will you require to accomplish other objectives?
- Family: Would you like to have children? In that case, how do you plan to parent well? In what way do you want your partner or your extended family to see you?
- Artistic: Do you have any artistic objectives?
- Attitude: Is there anything preventing you from reaching your goals? Is there anything in your behavior that irritates you? (If yes, make a goal to change your behavior or figure out how to solve the issue.)
- Physical: Do you have any sports aspirations? Do you want to be in good health well into old age? How are you going to go about doing this?

- Pleasure: What kind of fun do you wish to have? (You ought to make sure that a portion of your existence is your own!)
- Public Service: Are you interested in improving the world? If so, how?

After giving these ideas considerable thought, choose one or more goals from each category that most accurately represent your objectives. Next, think about pruning once more to get down to a manageable amount of truly important goals.

While doing this, be sure that the objectives you have established are ones that you actually want to accomplish rather than ones that your employers, family, or parents may think are appropriate. (If you have a spouse, you should definitely think about what they desire, but don't forget to stay true to yourself as well!)

Step 2: Make Smaller Objectives

Establish a five-year plan comprising of smaller goals that you must accomplish in order to reach your lifetime plan after you have determined your lifetime goals.

Next, make plans for the next year, the next six months, and the next month that include ever smaller targets that you need to meet in order to fulfill your lifetime objectives. Every one of these ought to be predicated on the prior scheme.

Next, make a daily to-do list of the tasks you need to complete in order to move closer to your long-term objectives.

Your initial, smaller goals can be to read books and learn about the accomplishment of your higher level objectives. This will assist you in raising the caliber and realistic level of your goal-setting.

In conclusion, go over your plans to ensure they align with your desired lifestyle.

Maintaining Direction

After you've selected your initial set of objectives, continue the process by going over and making updates to your To-Do List every day.

Regularly review and modify the longer-term goals to reflect your changing priorities and experiences. (Using a computer-based diary to plan recurring, frequent evaluations is an effective approach to accomplish this.)

SMART Objectives

Using the SMART acronym is a helpful strategy to increase the impact of your goals. Although there are several variations (some included in parenthesis), SMART often stands for:

S: Specific, or Significant.
M: Measurable, also known as meaningful.
A: Achievable (or focused on taking action).
R: Rewarding or Relevant.
T: Temporary (or Observable).

For instance, using the SMART goal "To have completed my trip around the world by December 31, 2027" is more effective than setting the objective "to sail around the world." It goes without saying that only with extensive prior planning will this be possible!

Additional Goal-Setting Advice

You can create goals that are both practical and attainable by using the general ideas listed below:

- Declare each objective in a constructive manner. State your objectives in a positive manner. It is far preferable to aim for "Execute this technique well" rather than "Don't make this stupid mistake."
- To be exact – Establish clear objectives with dates, times, and sums so that you can track your progress. By doing this, you'll be able to recognize when the goal has been reached and feel completely satisfied with your accomplishment.
- Establish priorities. As you have multiple objectives, assign a priority to each. This helps you focus on the most crucial goals and keeps you from becoming overwhelmed by having too many.
- Setting goals in writing helps them become more concrete and powerful.
- Set modest operational goals. Make sure the low-level objectives you're aiming for are manageable and compact. An overly ambitious objective may give the impression that you are not moving in the right direction. Setting modest, gradual goals increases the likelihood of success.

- Establish performance goals rather than outcome goals: Be sure to choose objectives that provide you the greatest amount of control. When outside factors prevent you from accomplishing a personal objective, it can be very disheartening! In the business world, these could be unanticipated consequences of government action or unfavorable corporate circumstances. In sports, these could include bad judgment, unfavorable circumstances, injuries, or just plain bad luck. If your objectives are dependent on your own performance, you will be responsible for their achievement and able to partake in the rewards.
- Make sure your goals are achievable by setting realistic objectives. A wide range of individuals (such as employers, parents, the media, or society at large) may establish unattainable standards for you. They frequently act in this way without considering your own goals and aspirations. Setting too challenging of goals is also a possibility since you might not recognize the challenges along the road or realize the precise amount of

talent you need to acquire to reach a given performance level.

Reaching Objectives
Spend some time basking in the happiness that comes from accomplishing a goal. Consider the ramifications of reaching the goal and note your advancement toward other objectives.

Give yourself a suitable reward if the aim was important. You gain the self-assurance you deserve with the help of all of this.

Now that you've accomplished this objective, go over the remaining goal plans:

- Make your next objective harder if the last one was too easy to accomplish.
- If achieving the objective took a depressingly long time, ease up on the next one.
- Change your goals if you learn something that might lead you to do so.
- If, despite reaching the goal, you felt that you lacked some talents, consider whether to create new objectives to address this.

Repurpose the lessons you've learned to inform the way you define your future objectives. Additionally, keep in mind that your objectives will evolve over time. Regularly adjust them to reflect your growing knowledge and experience. If your goals are no longer motivating, you might want to consider letting them go.

An Illustration of Personal Objectives
Susan has made the decision to reflect on her life goals as her New Year's Resolution.

Her long-term objectives are as follows:

- My career goal is "To be managing editor of the magazine that I work for."
- Creative: "To continue honing my illustration techniques. My ultimate goal is to have a solo exhibition at our downtown gallery."
- Regarding the body, "to run a marathon."

After enumerating her lifelong objectives, Susan divides each one into more doable, smaller objectives.

Let's examine more closely how she might achieve her lifetime professional ambition of managing her magazine:

- Over five years, I want to "become deputy editor."
- A one-year objective: "Offer to help with projects that the managing editor is currently in charge of."
- "Go back to school and finish my journalism degree" is the six-month aim.
- Goal for the first month: "Talk to the current managing editor to determine what skills are needed to do the job."
- One-week Goal to "book the meeting with the managing editor."

This example demonstrates how setting smaller, more achievable goals helps to clarify how larger objectives will be achieved.

The advantages of establishing goals

While setting goals is a standard activity in many aspects of life, it is frequently disregarded in terms of success and personal growth. This can be the case because creating goals can be intimidating, or it might be the case that we are unaware of all the advantages.

Setting objectives provides you with something to strive for, which is one of its most evident advantages. In the absence of objectives, it's simple to become mired in the routine and forget your life's purpose. You feel more purposeful and inspired to keep going forward when you have definite goals to work for.

Setting goals also keeps you focused and organized, which is a huge advantage. Pursuing achievement in the absence of well-defined objectives is akin to attempting to hit an invisible target. It's possible that you'll get lucky and do something amazing, but more usually than not, you'll just feel lost and dissatisfied.

However, you may create a plan of action and break down the necessary stages to reach specific goals when you have them in mind. Knowing precisely what has to be done when increases the likelihood that you will accomplish your goals.

And last, goal-setting can help you become more disciplined and adept at time management. You must develop superior time and resource management skills if you want to pursue your goals, which call for commitment and attention. These are useful abilities that will help you not only in reaching your objectives but in every aspect of your life.

As you can see, goal-setting has a lot of advantages. Thus, now is the perfect moment to begin utilizing this effective instrument if you haven't previously in order to help you succeed.

Recall that the secret to making goals that work is to start modest and work your way up to more challenging ones as you start to see results. As you continue to work toward your ultimate objective, this will keep you motivated and prevent you from becoming overwhelmed.

Why should you put your objectives in writing?
If you want to do anything in life, setting goals is essential. But why is it so crucial to put your goals in writing?
Some may argue that it is useless to write down your goals since you can simply forget about them or

never look at them again. In actuality, though, one of the most crucial things you can do to increase your chances of success is to put your goals in paper.

This is the reason why:

1. It holds you responsible.
You're effectively promising yourself that you'll go above and beyond to accomplish your goals when you put them in writing. Maintaining this sense of accountability is essential if you wish to achieve your objectives.

2. It provides you with understanding.
Writing down your objectives makes you reflect on what it is that you truly want to accomplish. You need this clarity in order to create a plan of action that will enable you to achieve your objectives.

3. It sustains your motivation
Having your objectives in front of you on paper can serve as a powerful motivation. Your objectives will serve as a constant reminder of your objectives and the reasons they are significant to you. This will support your ability to maintain focus and motivation in the face of adversity.

4. It gives your objectives greater heft.
Your ambitions may appear to be nothing more than pipe dreams when they are only ideas in your mind. But they take on a solid, genuine quality when they are put in writing. This may strengthen your conviction that reaching your objectives is genuinely feasible.

5. It lets you monitor your development
Setting down your objectives enables you to monitor your development over time. You are able to observe your progress and how much nearer you are to reaching your objectives. This can be an excellent strategy for maintaining motivation and making progress.

So make sure to put your goals in writing if you're serious about accomplishing them. This small deed can go a long way toward assisting you in reaching your goal.

The influence of optimistic thinking
The ability to think positively is crucial for creating and accomplishing goals. Individuals who approach

goal-setting and achievement with optimism are more likely to succeed than those who don't.

When it comes to creating and accomplishing goals, positive thinking is crucial for several reasons. To start with, optimistic thinkers are more likely to move toward their objectives. Additionally, they are more inclined to keep going when things get hard and to view setbacks as transient rather than irreversible.

Positive thinking can also make you feel more confident and motivated. You're more likely to make the required sacrifices and maintain focus on your goals when you have confidence in your own abilities to reach your goals.

Lastly, you can draw fortunate events and people into your life by keeping an optimistic outlook on goal-setting and achievement. When you exude self-assurance and optimism, others are more inclined to want to assist you in realizing your objectives.

Thus, keep an optimistic mindset if you're serious about creating and reaching your goals!

Overcoming challenges

It's crucial to keep in mind that you will run into challenges when creating goals. It is unavoidable. The secret is to avoid letting these hindrances prevent you from succeeding. Here are some pointers on overcoming challenges and accomplishing your objectives:

1. Identify your objective

Ascertaining that your aim is specific and well-defined is the first step. What goal do you have in mind? Be precise and record it in writing. When times are hard, this will support your ability to remain motivated and focused.

2. Have confidence in oneself

You have to have faith in your ability to succeed. Though it may seem obvious, this is crucial. If you don't, nobody else will have faith in you. Thus, be sure that you believe that you can accomplish your objective.

3. Make a strategy

After you've determined your objective, you need to draft an action plan. What actions are necessary for you to accomplish your goal? Create a list and place it in a visible location for each day. It will assist you in staying on course.

4. Act

The most crucial thing to do is to act. Don't wait for things to happen while you sit there. It is crucial to start, even if you just make modest progress at first. You'll be closer to reaching your objective the sooner you act.

5. Get beyond obstacles

You will experience difficulties from time to time. If things don't go as planned, you might want to give up. It's critical to keep in mind that these difficulties are just transient. They neither define you nor your objective. Recuperate yourself and proceed.

6. Remain Dogged

Attaining your objective will need perseverance, hard effort, and commitment. But in the end, it will be worthwhile. Thus, keep going even when things get difficult. Keep going and don't give up until you accomplish your objective.

7. Honor your accomplishments
Celebrate your accomplishment when you've reached your goal. It's a great accomplishment, and you ought to feel proud. After then, focus on your next objective and repeat the process.

Never give up on your aspirations
The majority of people dream. aspirations to change the world, become affluent, and travel. But a great deal of people never fulfill their aspirations. They seldom take the time to concentrate on what they truly want because they are too caught up in the daily grind.

You must establish goals if you wish to realize your aspirations. Setting goals is the act of determining what you want to accomplish and then making the required moves to get there.

Setting objectives gives you something to aim toward. You have a goal or objective to strive toward. You are just aimlessly floating through life if you don't have any ambitions.

Planning and dedication are necessary for goal achievement. You must choose an objective that is both doable and reasonable. After deciding on your objective, you must plan how you will get there. There may be some investigation and introspection involved with this.

You must make a commitment to your plan and goal once you have them. This entails moving toward your objective. It entails giving up something and going above and beyond to accomplish your objective.

Never surrender your aspirations. If something is something you truly want, you will find a method to make it happen. The first step to realizing your aspirations is to set goals. Thus, why do you delay? Make a positive impact in your life by starting to create objectives today.

CHAPTER 3
WE GET MORE WHEN WE GIVE

There is a proverb in Chinese that reads, "Nap for an hour and you will be happy." Go fishing if you want joy for a day. To get joy for a year, acquire a fortune. Assisting someone will bring you satisfaction for a lifetime. The best intellectuals have proposed the same idea for centuries: serving others brings happiness.

Because we receive by giving, as Saint Francis of Assisi once said.

Winston Churchill once said, "We make a living by what we get; we make a life by what we give."

Nobel Peace Prize winner: "Making money is a form of happiness; making other people happy is a super happiness." Yunus Muhammad

Giving back gives you a purpose, which benefits both you and the people you are helping. A purpose-driven existence leads to a happy individual, according to Goldie Hawn.

Thus, we are taught early on that giving is preferable to receiving. We are instilled with the old proverb from the moment we eat our first piece of birthday cake together. But does the truism have a deeper meaning?

The answer is unquestionably yes. Giving is a potent means of achieving personal development and long-term happiness, as anecdotal evidence suggests. Scientific study offers strong evidence to support this theory. We now know that giving engages the same brain regions that are excited by food and sex thanks to fMRI technology. Research indicates that generosity is ingrained in the brain and is rewarding. It's possible that leading a happier, healthier, wealthier, more productive, and meaningful life is all due to helping others.

However, it's crucial to keep in mind that giving isn't always rewarding. On the other hand, it's possible that giving can leave us feeling drained and used. These pointers can assist you in giving until it feels fantastic rather than until it hurts:

1. Discover your calling

Our generosity need to be based on our enthusiasm. What matters is the love we put into giving, not the amount we give. Naturally, we will be more concerned with this and less concerned with that, and that's okay. Selecting what is right for us should be the primary consideration, rather than just doing the morally correct thing.

2. Take some time

Giving someone your time can often be more meaningful for both the giver and the recipient than giving them money. Even if none of us is equally wealthy, we can all spare some of our free time to serve others. This time can be spent serving others for a few hours a day or a few days a year, or it can be dedicated to a lifetime of service.

3. Donate to organizations whose goals and outcomes are clear.

4. Look for methods to combine your passions and abilities with other people's needs.

According to Give & Take author Adam Grant, "selfless giving, in the absence of self-preservation instincts, easily becomes overwhelming." It's critical to be "otherish," which he characterizes as having a willingness to give more than take while maintaining awareness of your own needs.

5. Take the initiative rather than the passive route

Everybody has experienced the unease that arises from being forced to give, such when friends ask us to contribute to their fundraising efforts. Instead of giving out of compassion and generosity in these situations, we are more likely to do it in order to avoid embarrassment. Giving in this way is unlikely to make you feel good; instead, it's more likely to make you resentful. Rather, we ought to allocate some time, consider our alternatives, and choose the charity that most aligns with our ideals.

6. Avoid feeling obligated to donate.
Donating to worthy causes shouldn't be discouraged just because it doesn't always make us feel better. What an awful, greedy society this would be if all we had to do was give, just to get something back every time we did! However, the likelihood is that we won't be all that dedicated to the cause in the long run if we are feeling guilt-tripped into contributing.

Finding a strategy that works for us is crucial. When we do, our chances of finding happiness, meaning, and purpose in life—all of the things we strive for but find so challenging to achieve—increase with our level of giving.

Let me clarify that by giving, I do not always intend to give money. When it comes to an individual or an organization that provides important assistance to individuals, money may be a powerful tool for achieving many positive and constructive goals. I'm referring to service here, which is the time, effort, and energy we devote to aiding others and causes. Naturally, when we do that, we start to act as a positive force in the universe. We aid a neighbor, protect an additional acre of forest, and increase the opportunities and optimism in a community. We brighten someone's day. Mutual benefit is the evolutionary undercurrent at work here. Yes, we are assisting others, but we are also reaping unexpected benefits for ourselves.

Yes, we experience the pleasurable "helper's high," which is a surge of feel-good hormones like oxytocin. But that's really the tip of the iceberg. Volunteers performed higher on nine measures of emotional wellness, such as "personal independence, capacity for rich interpersonal relationships, and overall satisfaction with life," according to a United Health Group staff study (PDF). Most volunteers claimed to have experienced a reduction in stress, and almost all said that volunteering had improved their "sense of purpose in life."

Research has found significant benefits for older adults in particular. In a randomized clinical trial involving Baltimore's Experience Corps, Johns Hopkins researchers observed physical and cognitive benefits in older adult volunteers who tutored in urban schools. Participants reported significant gains in perceptions of social support and connectedness, as well as physical strength and mobility. Another Carnegie Mellon University study found volunteering was associated with a 40% lower risk of high blood pressure in older adults. It's possible the kind of volunteering can influence gains as well. Larger scale research out of Cornell University showed older adults who volunteered with an environmental stewardship program were less likely to experience depression in later years. The lower risk was 50% for environmental volunteers and 10% for non-environmental causes/services. Finally, research shows volunteerism significantly lowers mortality risk in one study by over 60%.

For all the focus on older adults, however, people in any age group experience advantages. Adolescents in a University of British Columbia study showed lower BMI, inflammation, and cholesterol readings following a ten week volunteer period. Emotional and physical changes appeared to go hand in hand.

As the director of the study noted, "[Those] who reported the greatest increases in empathy, altruistic behavior, and mental health were the ones who also saw the greatest improvements in their cardiovascular health."

The number of hours devoted to volunteering each week doesn't appear to influence most benefits, but the length of years does matter. As you can imagine, the longer you do it, the greater the benefit. Likewise, those who volunteer for self-focused reasons didn't benefit compared to non-volunteers. Apparently, we can intellectually know we'll benefit, but the advantages come when we let go of that intention.

It all makes perfect sense. Genuine giving isn't an act from the self as much as a participation in the world and relationships around us. Anthropologists who've studied modern hunter-gatherer groups explain how band members' identities are created through participation in the group. They become individuals within the context of the group, growing and accepted in relationship to the group, within an evolving give and take investment in the group.

I don't consider myself a religious person but was always intrigued by the idea of vocation put forth by writer and theologian Frederick Buechner: "Vocation is the place where our deep gladness meets the world's deep need." The happiest and most fulfilled people I know are those who feel they practice a vocation in life – whether or not it's how they earn their living.

We just aren't wired to have hours of time to wallow in chronic and ineffectual solipsism. Giving in whatever sense – formal volunteering, help to friends and neighbors, environmental work – helps us get out of our heads. A larger cause (even if it's just in a one-on-one exchange) than ourselves budges out the self-chatter. We can be in the moment and take "a vacation from our problems."

In an age when we build an online "profile" and stylize our image to our heart's (and ambition's) content, we can more than ever lose sight of where and how we're really made. We're not our assembled "likes" and "shares" or our crafted "timelines." We're not our collection of pithy tweets. We're our in-the-flesh contributions.

In giving of yourself – whether through parenthood, vocational service or other social commitments/relationships – I think you gain a certain confidence in your own worth and ability. We can chat ourselves up in our own minds from now until doomsday, but all the psychological pomp and primping is just grandiosity on its own. In acting and exchanging, in offering one's self and service – that's where the rubber meets the road. It's where we're truly tried and tested – where we grow. Ultimately, it illuminates the divide between grandiosity and gravitas.

We take the lessons – the perspective and humility and all the other goodies – back to our own lives. In the words of Norman Vincent Peale, "When you become detached mentally from yourself and concentrate on helping other people with their difficulties, you will be able to cope with your own more effectively. Somehow, the act of self-giving is a personal power-releasing factor." In part, the benefits come from our enhanced empathy. As author of The Power of Empathy, Katherine Ketcham, explains, those "who have high relational skills are more successful personally and professionally." We can be more effective in our work roles and emotional relationships. Overall, we enjoy a more fulfilling life and enhanced well-being. What could be more Primal than that?

CHAPTER 4
GIVE EVERY DOLLAR A JOB

One of the most difficult lessons I had to learn was the one that follows. Being a free spirit, I never thought I could accomplish this. However, following our year of unemployment and realizing how difficult our financial situation was, I was unable to keep track of every dollar's exact whereabouts.

One of the most crucial financial choices a person makes to organize their family's money is to Give Every dollar a Job. Yes, budgeting is back. After my last piece, you probably assumed I had forgotten about this taboo subject. I didn't.

What in the world does it mean to give our money a job when unemployment is on the rise and there are so many people looking for work?

We assign tasks to dollars, and each dollar in our budget must have one. There is a lot of flexibility in interpreting and determining what that means for your family.

All too frequently, when using traditional budgeting, one estimates the amount needed for each category based on previous year's spending and then expects that if we spend roughly the same amount, our budget would be balanced. It turns out to be a problem, and we don't know how we got so wrong.

It's too nebulous, even though we believe we have a plan and are being explicit.

A budget disaster is certain when large expenses like food, housing, insurance, cars, and other expenses are budgeted for and then there are very vague overflow categories like "savings" or "incidentals." I'm not sure about your family, but in ours, life is made up of a lot of little incidents, so using these two broad categories isn't practical. The secret is to dissect them and get very specific.

It could take months to create the ideal budget for your family; it must be worked out and revised over time. In the initial months, you will have to monitor and reassess each dollar. I strongly advise keeping a daily, weekly, and eventually monthly record of every dollar you spend if you're deeply in debt. While daily planning may seem excessive, the cost of your daily interest can be calculated, and 30 minutes a day of preparation can build up to a very tempting amount. You must be prepared to invest the necessary time in going back and rearranging those days as debt happened in just one day, plus one day, plus one day.

It takes some effort to find a budget that works for you. It requires being detailed, going beyond the surface, and giving your money clear direction. When you first work through your budget, make sure to allocate the extra $100. It needs to be given a job!

Budgets are ineffective because people have irrational expectations. When something is written down, doesn't it look so simple? According to the statements made before, the difficulty is in really sticking to the budget. (We'll discuss different approaches to make it work in a later post.)

For example, identify what "incidentals" mean and give them names. For parents, it could be the birthday celebrations to which their children are invited and the ensuing expectations regarding gifts. Really? Whoever sets aside that much money for those? You could get into problems for it. What about the nail that you stepped on last week and the tire that has to be replaced even though you recently replaced them a few months ago? There is more than one category for cars. We have a category called "our van is in serious trouble and will definitely need repairs." Breakdowns no longer surprise me, as much as it hurts to invest money in it. I hope I never have to use the "repairs" category, but if I do, it is available.

What about the category "savings"?
Identify "what the "task" of these savings is. Do you make investments? Reserve money for your ideal house addition?
Do you want to make one more mortgage payment a year? After that, assign those dollars a mission and, if you're doing it correctly, get them to work for you by bringing in more dollars. Savings might seem like an unattainable goal if you're just starting out, but don't worry—you'll succeed, and if you factor in these jobs, I'll jump for pleasure right there with you. Our dream front porch took us 17 years to create, but we paid cash for it and are now enjoying it.

Remember to give a distinct category to each and every solid dollar. The category you choose depends on how much of a priority it is in your budget.

Since every person is unique, you must be honest with yourself in order to make this budget work for you. "Starbucks" should be one category if you frequently prioritize treating yourself to a Starbucks indulgence. Don't just act as though you don't spend that much; instead, identify the category and make it a priority.

Establish a strict spending limit for the duration of the month and adhere to it. (This could surprise you.) My budget is heavily reliant on yard sales. I have categories for yard sales (spring/summer) and thrift stores (fall/winter). If I didn't, every Saturday morning, money would flow through my fingers since everything is so amazing. Even while I know that I frequently spend far more than that, I'm not going to pretend that $10 a week is a "good girl" amount and place it in that category. I've spent $50 a week, which may sound like a lot, but this is the point when you have to be honest with yourself about your spending, identify that as a category, and enter the amount that you will stick to—not just what you can afford to spend. If you find that to be $10 a week, then just take ten dollars in cash.

The money is gone when it's gone. No talks, no justifications.

This type of budgeting has the benefit of allowing you to account for every dollar you have allocated. Setting concrete goals and taking a seat to think over the numbers is incredibly beneficial because it involves active decision-making as opposed to passive observation. Rather than letting your financial circumstances dominate you, you are taking charge of them. Even when money is limited, you won't be caught off guard every month and forced to live in constant fear.

We have the next two largest spending months coming up. Now is the BEST time of year to get your hands dirty. Remorse is the last thing you want in January. Let's celebrate the new year with balloons and whistles instead of credit card and Visa statements.

Which Style Are you?
Individuals differ in how they relate to money. Some people are born savers, having extra cash at the end of the month. There are some that squander their money and have more months remaining in their budget. If you haven't already, keep a thirty-day journal of your expenditures to identify your spending habits. Keep track of your daily expenses

and purchases in a diary, log, or phone note. Keeping a record of your spending will support your next move.

Each and every dollar for a mission

It's likely that you've heard the advice to live on less than you earn. Once you are aware of your costs, record your income and make a monthly spending plan using a free budgeting application such as Orange Budget. Give each dollar you make a task. Make sure to budget for entertainment, shopping, and other sporadic expenses in addition to saving money. The objective is to develop a zero-balance budget, where each cent has a designated purpose and income less expenses equals zero. For more help, adhere to the financial guidelines.

Basics of Banking

One of the most crucial steps in laying the groundwork for your finances is selecting a bank or credit union. Before you start using any bank, take note of:

1. Convenience: Since a physical location makes transactions more accessible, it is usually easiest to work with a bank or credit union that is close to where you live or work.

Consider this while you are looking for banks or credit unions: How is the customer service?
- How accessible are the policies and what are the hours?
- Which would I rather use to pay my bills: online or via check?
- Which would I rather do: chat to someone face-to-face or utilize an app?
2. Cost: Steer clear of account fees. Overdraft fees, monthly maintenance fees, and ATM fees for taking out cash at an ATM that isn't connected to your bank are typical charges. The fee schedule provided by your bank or credit union details the various charges and fees. Make a note of it. As long as you keep your balance positive, several banks provide accounts that are free to use. Some may charge for services, and these costs may mount up over time. Before you sign up, make sure you are aware of all the charges related to your accounts.
3. Legitimacy: Verify that the organization you select is protected by the National Credit Union Administration (NCUA) for credit unions, or the Federal Deposit Insurance

Corporation (FDIC) for banks. To find choices in your area, use the NCUA Credit Union Finder or FDIC BankFind.

Once opened, a basic checking account will handle the majority of your everyday activities. However, you can use additional accounts, such as a money market account or basic savings account, to save for larger expenditures and emergency funds. Don't deposit money into any account you don't completely understand, and don't hesitate to ask questions. Find out more about credit unions versus banks.

Resources
- Banking Basics - Get solutions and answers for all your inquiries about bank accounts.
- Learn the distinctions between credit and debit cards so that you can create a spending plan.
- Orange Budget: Start creating a budget right now by using this free program.
- Federal Trade Commission Budget: Create your plan with the help of this free budgeting worksheet from the FTC.
- A well-liked online tool for budgeting is Mint.

- Another well-liked online budgeting tool is Every Dollar.

CHAPTER 5
AGE YOUR MONEY

Too many Americans are caught in the never-ending cycle of money coming in and money going out. They promptly reinvest almost every penny they make into covering their debts and other obligations. In fact, according to a CareerBuilder research, an astounding 78 percent of Americans live paycheck to paycheck.

For millions, the weekly or monthly cycle is tiresome. Since most Americans already have difficulty making ends meet, even a single unforeseen expense has the potential to put them in debt. Surely, there must be a solution.

Certain financial gurus believe that the age of your money has an impact on the solution. Not because it's printed, but rather because you purchased it. Your finances are more stable the older your money is, which enables you to save more money, and so on. Let's first discuss what your money's age actually represents before moving on.

"Aging" Financially

Essentially, the concept of aging your money is simply a modern interpretation of the age-old adage, which is to spend less than you make. Consider a piggy bank with a stopper on the bottom and a coin slot on top to get an idea of where age plays a role.

As you withdraw older funds from the bottom, the newly deposited funds remain on top. Your money becomes older the less you spend, so you can find yourself spending last month's money to pay this month's bills instead of this month's.

Letting money sit in your bank account for a while before spending it is the secret to saving. It's really easy to understand; all you have to do is set spending priorities. By creating and following a budget, you may reduce wasteful spending, increase your savings, and then watch as your money grows on its own. Setting goals can help you manage your budget because it will help you determine how much you must spend each month.

What Is the Minimum Age for Money?

Since every person's financial circumstances are unique, there is no one right answer to this topic, but in general, you want your money to be at least a month old. The whole point of ageing your money is to create a sense of security, so your money is genuinely old enough when you feel comfortable enough about your finances.

Naturally, there is such a thing as having too much money. It's wise to save for long-term objectives like retirement, but that doesn't mean you have to give up on short-term objectives as well. You should also feel a little more confidence in your abilities to plan a vacation or indulge in presents once you've saved up and have a more comfortable future.

Creating Long-Term Stability in Finances
Aging your money is all about positioning yourself for a better financial future, just like any other budgeting technique. You continually increase the amount of money in your financial safety net by using older money and then adding newer money on top. It takes a lot of work to plan your spending, set goals, and adhere to a budget, but doing so is the greatest way to age your money and get ready for the future.

Retirement should be your ultimate aim, and managing your money as you get older can reduce stress. Spending less than you make is the key to ageing your cash, however after retirement, your wages will likely decline but your spending may not. Aging your money is a simple approach to make sure you have a more solid financial picture, even if retirement planning is generally more complicated.

Making a budget doesn't have to be difficult or take up a lot of your day. In actuality, the simplest budgeting strategies are frequently the best. Consider the 50/30/20 rule, for instance. The 50/30/20 rule is a simple monthly budgeting technique that provides you with precise monthly allocations for savings and living expenses.

You can securely prevent overspending and gradually increase your savings with a clear monthly budget summary, all without having to laboriously track every transaction.

Therefore, you might consider trying the 50/30/20 strategy if you have ever downloaded a budgeting app but then gave it up after the third day. Here's how it functions—it's one of the better budgeting suggestions we've discovered.

What is the rule of 50/30/20?
A straightforward budgeting technique that will assist you in efficiently, easily, and sustainably managing your finances is the 50/30/20 rule. Generally speaking, you should set aside 50% of your monthly after-tax income for needs, 30% for wants, and 20% for savings or debt repayment.

You may make better use of your finances by consistently maintaining a balance between these primary spending categories. Additionally, you can spare yourself the time and anxiety of constantly having to delve into the specifics because there are only three main areas to keep care of.

The 50/30/20 rule should only be applied as a general guideline when creating a budget, though. The precise percentages for each category vary depending on a number of factors, including inflation, the cost of living in your area, and your own financial status.

When it comes to budgeting, a common query is "Why can't I save more?" The 50/30/20 rule is a fantastic method to tackle this age-old conundrum and give your spending habits more structure. It can facilitate the achievement of your financial objectives, including debt repayment and rainy-day savings.

The 50/30/20 rule: whence did it originate?
The authors of "All Your Worth: The Ultimate Lifetime Money Plan," a 2005 book co-authored by current US Senator Elizabeth Warren and her daughter Amelia Warren Tyagi, are the source of the 50/30/20 rule.

Warren and Tyagi draw the conclusion that you don't need a complex budget to get your money in order, citing more than 20 years of research. All you have to do is apply the 50/30/20 rule to allocate your funds among your needs, wants, and savings objectives.

How to create a budget using the 50/30/20 guideline

By separating your after-tax income into just three spending categories—needs, wants, and savings or debts—the 50/30/20 rule makes budgeting easier.

It will be simpler to stay within your budget and control your spending if you know exactly how much to spend in each category. The following is an example of a budget that follows the 50/30/20 rule:

Give necessities 50% of your income

Put simply, needs are the costs you cannot avoid—the payments for all the necessities that make life unpleasant. Your most essential expenses should be paid for using half of your after-tax income.

Needs could consist of:

- Rent each month
- Bills for gas and electricity
- Insurances for transportation (healthcare, auto, pet)
- Minimum payments due on loans
- Basic food

For instance, €1000 of your monthly after-tax income of €2000 should go toward meeting your necessities.

Each person's budget may be different from this one. Should you discover that your needs exceed fifty percent of your take-home pay, you might be able to reduce those costs somewhat by making certain adjustments. Changing electricity providers or coming up with new ways to shop more cheaply for groceries could take care of this. It might also indicate more significant life adjustments, like searching for a less costly place to live.

You should allocate thirty percent of your income towards desires

Thirty percent of your after-tax income can be allocated to wants, with the remaining fifty percent going toward meeting your most basic requirements. Non-essential expenses, or items you choose to spend money on even though you could live without them, are referred to as wants.

These could consist of:

- Eating out
- Shopping for clothes
- Vacations
- Fitness memberships
- Subscriptions to media (Netflix, HBO, Amazon Prime)
- Groceries (apart from the necessities)

Using the same example as before, you can spend €600 on wants if your monthly after-tax income is €2000. Additionally, it's wise to consider which of your wants you could give up if you find that you're spending too much on them.

It should be noted that living by the 50/30/20 guideline does not preclude enjoying life. It just involves identifying areas of your budget where you're unnecessarily overspending and becoming more frugal with your money. Asking yourself if you could live without something will help you determine if it's a need or a want. That's most likely a want if the response is yes.

Leave 20% of your income in savings.

After deducting 30% of your monthly income from your wants and 50% from your requirements, you can use the remaining 20% of your income to pay off debt or reach your savings targets. Even if the minimal payments are regarded as necessities, any more payments are categorized as saves because they lower your current debt and future interest.

Setting aside 20% of your monthly income on a regular basis will help you create a stronger, longer-lasting savings plan. This is true whether your ultimate objective is to save for a down payment on a home, create a long-term personal financial strategy, or simply accumulate an emergency fund.

And the rate at which the savings may accumulate is astounding. You may allocate €400 of your monthly take-home pay—€2000 after taxes—to your savings objectives. You'll have saved around €5000 in a year!

Using the 50/30/20 rule: a comprehensive guide
So what is the real application of the 50/30/20 rule? You must classify your spending and determine the

50/30/20 ratio based on your income in order to use this straightforward budgeting guideline. Here's how to do it:

1. Determine your income after taxes.

To apply the 50/30/20 budgeting guideline, figure out your income after taxes. If you work as a freelancer, your monthly earnings less your business expenses and the amount you have set up for taxes will be your after-tax income.

This will be simpler if you are an employee who receives a consistent paycheck. Check the amount that appears in your bank account each month by looking at your payslip. Re-add any automatic deductions from your salary, such as health insurance or pension contributions.

2. Sort the money you spent during the previous month.

You must examine how and where you have spent your revenue for the past month in order to obtain an accurate picture of where your money is going each month. Get a copy of your last 30 days' worth of bank statements, or just use the N26 app's Insights function. All of your transactions are automatically sorted into categories like Pay, Grocery & Food, Entertainment & Leisure, and more.

Sort all of your spending into three categories: savings, wants, and needs. Recall that a need is a necessary expense—like rent—that you cannot live without. An extra indulgence, like eating out, that you could live without is called a want. Furthermore, saves might be defined as extra debt repayments, pension fund contributions made in retirement, or rainy-day funds.

3. Assess and modify your expenditures to align with the 50/30/20 rule.
Now that you know how much of your monthly income is allocated to savings, requirements, and wants, you can begin modifying your spending plan to adhere to the 50/30/20 guideline. Calculating how much you spend each month on your wants is the greatest method to do this.

The 50/30/20 guideline states that a want is just a basic courtesy that lets you enjoy life, not something extravagant. Determining which of your wants you can give up is the greatest way to keep within 30% of your take-home pay, as cutting back on your necessities can be a difficult and complicated undertaking. Your chances of reaching your 20% savings goal increase with the amount you cut back on wants.

Spreadsheet with the 50/30/20 rules
If you would want to build a more detailed budget, a 50/30/20 rule spreadsheet is an excellent choice, even though our 50/30/20 rule calculator can give you a broad sense of your ideal 50/30/20 rule budget.

Spreadsheet budgeting is made simpler by the prepared templates available in spreadsheet programs like Microsoft Excel, Google Sheets, and Apple Numbers. Spreadsheets for the 50/30/20 rule are widely available for free online, and they work with any program you're using.

Automate the 50/30/20 rule using N26
You can feel more confident and in charge of your financial situation by using budgeting techniques. Having financial instruments that can support you along the journey is also beneficial. N26 wants to make it easy for you to accomplish your financial objectives. With a 100% mobile bank account, you

can access your money from anywhere and receive real-time push notifications to keep an eye on your finances.

Additionally, you can monitor several savings goals with your free Spaces sub-accounts, and N26 Insights will automatically categorize your spending for you to help you stay on track.

CHAPTER 6
TEACHING YOUR KIDS TO BUDGET

Setting a budget. It's a skill that will help your children manage their finances and prepare them for a sound financial future. Plus, the earlier your kids learn to budget, the better, since financial habits are formed by the time they are seven years old.

Fortunately, financial lessons for children don't have to be dry and boring. There are numerous enjoyable ways to support their education. For advice on teaching kids about budgeting, games and activities to practice budgeting, and more, keep reading.

What is the purpose of budgeting?

Financial planning is referred to as budgeting. A budget is a strategy that assists you in monitoring every dollar that enters your account (your revenue) and every dollar that leaves it (your expenses).

You take charge of your money when you create a budget, whether it's for a specific occasion, a week, or a month. In essence, you're giving your money instructions. If you don't have a budget, you could wonder where the money went.

Why it's crucial to teach budgeting to your children

Giving your children a budget early on helps them take financial responsibility. It aids in their understanding that finances are finite. They must therefore decide how much to spend and how much to save depending on their financial situation.

Before balancing home expenditures and mortgage repayments on a wage as an adult, budgeting is a useful skill to acquire early. Youngsters who practice budgeting are less likely to incur debt in the future.

Kids will need to learn how to budget throughout their life. It goes beyond money. According to Beth Zemble, VP of Education at GoHenry, "budgeting also introduces life lessons like patience, planning ahead, smart decision-making, and sharing." "You're preparing your children for sound financial habits later in life by teaching them how to budget for needs, wants, and savings at a young age."

How to easily teach children about budgeting

A plan that makes it easier for your child to get more out of their money is the easiest method to teach them about budgeting. With the aid of a budget, individuals may see exactly how much money they have to work with and accelerate the process of saving money.

Talk to your child about how making a budget will help them make sure they have enough money to fulfill their needs and wants if they are having trouble saving their allowance for the entire week. It implies that their financial needs won't be met suddenly.

You may argue that adults need to budget for the same reasons. Every year, the president must draft the government's budget and present it to Congress. Showing rather than telling your children about budgeting may help them understand it better.

Teach your children about budgeting.
When you next go down to balance your budget, have your kids sit alongside you and go through it together to teach them how budgeting works. Alternatively, show them your monthly outgoings using a bank statement.

Describe the necessity of making sure you have adequate cash on hand to pay for necessities like lighting and heating. However, you also need to budget for necessities like gas and food.

Talk about how much is left over for eating out or vacations. Next, find out how much you can put aside each month for a long-term savings objective, such as a trip or a new automobile.

It could be a good idea to discuss with your children what occurs when your budget isn't large enough to cover necessities. There will be a chance to discuss debt and how interest increases the cost of borrowing.
However, since children learn best via doing, here are some more teaching methods.

Ways to introduce children to budgeting
Finding lessons to teach your children about money can be challenging. But it's never too early to teach your kids to budget, since many get an allowance as early as age six. The fundamentals are understandable to kids as young as three.

- Our top picks for instructing children about budgeting
- Spending limit on candy purchases

- Play games that help you budget.
- Control your grocery spending.
- Set aside money for a specific occasion
- Control a grant
- Give, spend, or save envelopes.
- Give, spend, or save jars.
- Utilize a template or budget worksheet.
- Show them a kid-friendly money management app.

Spending limit on candy purchases

A small child can be given a certain amount of money to spend on candies. Allow them to decide whether to purchase multiple smaller candies or splurge on a single, enormous chocolate bar.

Play games that help you budget

You can teach your children about budgeting by using any of the many available budgeting games. Using counters or beads is a good one. Let's say the beads stand for income, and then designate other outgoings or expenses on jars or bowls. For smaller children, keep it simple: "rent," "food," "savings," and "fun money."

Make them fill jars with the appropriate quantity for savings and needs first. Allow them to then fill the fun money jar with the remaining amount. Use it as a chance to explain the 50-30-20 rule to older kids. (30% wants, 20% savings, and 50% needs).

Teach your children how to add an unexpected item to their budget. Give your youngster some paper and some scenarios to illustrate, such as receiving a bonus at work, losing their job, or purchasing a car. Assist them in determining where to make cuts and what to do with an unforeseen windfall.

Control your grocery spending

Assign your youngster the task of managing the weekly budget for grocery shopping. Assist them in compiling a list of the foods you require and compare prices at the store. Ask them to tally up and check that the amount stays within the allocated funds.

A special event budget

Give your youngster budget control if you're planning a family day. Verify if the price of parking, gas, and food has been included.

Alternatively, include them in your vacation savings efforts. Inform them of your savings and the remaining expenses that need to be planned for. Ask them to suggest some additional sources of income so you can meet your savings target.

Control a grant

A child's allowance is an excellent teaching tool for money management. They will be given a weekly budget to work with. They choose where it goes and how to prolong it. An allowance each month will teach older children how to stretch their money farther over longer time periods.

Your children will be able to increase their income if you want to compensate them for performing extra tasks. It will also assist students in understanding the connection between money and labor.

Give, spend, or save envelopes

Give your children three envelopes: Give, Save, and Spend. You might ask your children to draw or paint whatever they like on the envelopes. Make them split their allowance between the envelopes each time they receive it.

Assume that their weekly allotment is $5. They deposit two dollars in the Spend envelope, two in the Save envelope, and one dollar in the Give envelope the day they are paid. It's simple, yet even for six-year-olds, it works.

Give, spend, or save jars
Younger children might benefit more from splitting their money among jars. They can actually see their pennies and dollar notes add up, but the idea remains the same. that they will always be aware of their possessions.

Make the system easy to use. A jar to hold inexpensive goods, such as little toys or candies. Plus an additional, larger jar for rewards, like larger toys or games, that they are now unable to purchase.

Utilize a template or budget worksheet
Your children might scoff at this one. However, some people find it very appealing to be able to arrange their statistics into pre-made columns. It doesn't have to be an intricate online spreadsheet with formulas (though math-savvy, tech-savvy teenagers might find this entertaining). All you need

is a basic template that you can download and have your youngster fill out.

Show them a kid-friendly money management app

Your children may learn a lot about budgeting by using GoHenry's in-app Money Missions feature. For every age, there are interactive games, quizzes, bite-sized courses, and films. They'll pick up additional practical money management skills like investing, saving, and prudent spending in addition to budgeting.

Your adolescent may feel tempted to spend money on expensive coffee with pals, a new clothing that's in style, and another dinner out to celebrate a friend's birthday. Then, before they realize it, they've spent all of their money and are unable to get the data plan they had been saving for. However, they will have a plan for how to spend and save their money if they have a budget in place. Additionally, budgeting can assist children and teenagers develop money management skills that will benefit them far into adulthood. The main advantage of having a personal budget is that, with proper planning, they should always have enough money to pay for the necessities and, ideally, have some more to purchase the items they desire.

Furthermore, it's important for young children to understand how much things cost—like a desired toy—and whether they have the money to pay for them, even if you might not force them to sit through the process of developing a budget for your household's costs. Will it be covered by their allowance? As they get older, youngsters might learn how to save money and start saving up for something greater, like a new gaming station.

When children are taught how to budget early on, they will develop into teens and eventually adults who know how to manage their personal finances and save money.

Five steps to help kids develop a budget
1. Determine their "income" (also known as allowance).
Suppose you had no hoop to shoot into and no ball to bounce about if you wanted to learn how to play basketball. When you don't have any money, learning about money is like this: it's simply theoretical and not really useful. Giving your

children or teenagers some cash to practice with is one method to help them learn how to manage their finances.

Giving your children an allowance is a smart way to give them a consistent "income," regardless of their age. While some experts recommend that the child's age should match the weekly allowance in dollars, you should perform the math with our allowance calculator to see what works best for your household.

The key takeaway is that funds must arrive before they depart, and your youngster needs a certain amount of money to work with when creating a budget.

2. Determine the fixed and variable expenses.
You might wonder, "What typical kid has fixed and variable expenses." Your tween or adolescent will probably have fixed and variable bills that they need to pay even though they aren't paying off a mortgage. Extracurricular activities, a monthly phone bill, or occasionally purchasing lunch at the mall can all be excellent methods to distinguish fixed from variable spending.

To put it succinctly, you want children to learn that a fixed cost is an amount of money that is paid in advance for a certain commodity or service, for which you know the whole amount and the date of payment. Teens who budget for this now will be better prepared for the day when they must pay fixed costs to live independently or obtain auto insurance.

Then impart to your child the priceless gift of living outside of the red later in life. Teach them how knowing what's left over in the budget for variable expenses comes from making forward plans and paying bills on time to avoid late fines.

3. Talk about the distinction between wants and needs.
Being a child is definitely great. In their context, spending money and covering "variable" costs are frequently synonymous. (Don't be upset with them for this luxury; they will eventually have to pay for home maintenance and utility bills.)

Differentiating between necessities and wants is a challenge that children of all ages face. Although you've certainly got some experience realizing when you don't need another black dress, kids and teenagers aren't always the best at exercising self control. (Do you recall the days when your life would end if you didn't own the same pair of brand-new, stylish shoes as all your friends? After several decades, not much has changed.)

High school is not always easy. Some children view those new shoes as somewhat necessary. It's alright. The key is to help your tween fashionista comprehend value in addition to cost; if she truly needs those shoes, she will have to set aside money and create a budget for them.

Should that seem like too much work (and your child quickly forgets why those shoes were so amazing in the first place), perhaps it was only a passing fancy. In any case, a valuable lesson can be learned.

4. Help your kids establish savings objectives (or apply the 50/30/20 rule).
A budget should be based on needs (50%), wants (30%), and savings (20%).
Alright, so your child is enthusiastic about the shoes and is prepared to work for them. Not only is this a

terrific opportunity for you to teach about short- and long-term savings, but it also has an inherent "goal." Well, the shoes are temporary, but what about in the long run? Remind your adolescent how amazing it would be to buy their first car, cover their own tuition for a year of college, or actually take that gap year trip to Europe. Don't be afraid to do these things.

Finding the sweet spot between now, tomorrow, and the future is the ultimate goal of money management; even the most astute financial advisors must constantly strike this balance. A teenager's version of this is more like today, the weekend, and summer vacation, whereas parents' versions tend to be today, the end of the month, and retirement.

The idea is that everyone distributes resources, time, and effort pretty much in the same way. This is known as the 50/30/20 budgeting rule by experts, and it's a fantastic model to educate your children. They will discover the appropriate amount of money to spend as well as the importance and propriety of indulging in pleasure and enjoyment throughout this lifetime. However, setting aside a small sum of money on a regular basis to invest in your future self is also quite smart. When you are able to accomplish all three at once, spending money will feel easy and productive rather than stressful or wasteful.

5. Select the categories for your budget and the portion of your money that will go into each.
Congratulations! This lesson has come to a close, and now you and your financially astute child can embark on a real-life budgeting journey. This is the moment to allocate a portion of the overall amount to each category after dividing the allowance or revenue into them.

It's a wonderful smart habit to start saving 20% of your salary right away; you'll thank me later. Younger children fare better with a jar than a traditional piggy bank since they can see the pennies constantly adding up. (Just make a tiny incision in the lid, and don't forget to tightly shut it.) Putting that twenty percent straight into an online savings account, where they can watch interest build, is more likely to impress them. Gratuitous cash!

Take a step back and let your child create a list of budget categories that are important to them, such as clothes, toys, entertainment, snacks, stylish shoes, and even an Xbox, as long as they fulfill their half of the bargain and save a little money. Remember about significant occasions like budgeting for prom or the holidays! It's unlikely that what matters to them matters to you, but that's not the point. You're teaching children that things are expensive, that one must work for one's money, that no one can have everything they want when they want it, and that they should make thoughtful decisions.

That is an invaluable lesson in money management. Well done, you.

CHAPTER 7
GET READY TO INVEST

Growth is one of the most essential aspects of life that investing can promote. Investing may therefore be the key to gaining these freedoms if you're hoping to accumulate long-term wealth and establish the financial means to accomplish lifelong goals. We've compiled a summary of what investing is, what people invest in, how people invest, and what you might need to get started to get you started.

Investing: What is it?

Whether we realize it or not, we devote a lot of time and attention to learning new skills throughout our lives—whether it's attending college or mastering a new recipe. We frequently do these actions with the expectation that they will benefit us later on, like when we graduate from college and get our ideal job. The idea is essentially similar when it comes to the financial aspect of investing: you invest money in something with the hope of making money later on.

An investment return is the term used to describe the profit you make from financial investments, and it is typically stated as a percentage. For instance, if you invest €1,000 and receive €1,100 at the conclusion of the investment period, you have made a profit of €100, or 10% of your initial investment.

What motivates people to invest?
People have used investment as a way to accumulate money for hundreds of years. Compound growth is the main factor behind the effectiveness of long-term investing. When investment gains are reinvested, they compound, or get greater and bigger, which speeds up the process of reaching your financial objectives. Your funds will increase more quickly each year if, for instance, you invest €100 a month at an 8% interest rate for the following 20 years. The idea is that you will wind up with a lot more money at the conclusion of the investing period than you would have if you had put the same amount into a savings account.

For a lot of people, this means having the money to pay for retirement, cars, travel, schooling, homeownership, and so forth! Therefore, because investing can present prospects, people frequently turn to it.

Investing versus saving

The goal of saving is to keep money liquid so that it is available when needed. For instance, if you saved €50 per week for the following five years, you would have the money ready when that time came to an end. Savings usually yields no return because there is virtually little risk (inflation can lead returns on even interest-bearing savings accounts to be negative).

In contrast, when you invest, you can anticipate a return on your investment; yet, there's also a potential that you won't make any profit or receive a return on your entire investment. However, investing tactics (which we'll cover later in this article) can help handle this unpredictability.

Generally speaking, an investment's potential return increases with its risk. This is due to the fact that, as an investor, your profit (return) is typically determined by the degree of risk associated with an investment—a concept known as the risk and return tradeoff.

Although the terms trading and investing are frequently used synonymously, they are not the same. The main goal of investing is to produce investment returns over an extended length of time. This type of investing is already used by a large number of people through government-run retirement plans. Trading, on the other hand, is more concerned with making quick profits by buying and selling investments often. Furthermore, there is speculative investing, which entails very high levels of risk and hence extremely unpredictable future profits.

Who makes up the average investor?
There are two primary categories of investors: institutional (such as businesses or organizations) and private (common people). Together, these investors make trillions of euros in investments around Europe each year. Over 50 million individual investors and 21 million families invest their money in Germany alone1. France, the Netherlands, Italy, and Luxembourg are among the other nations having a high concentration of private investors1.

What do individuals typically invest in?
An asset is something that you own that has worth and can be exchanged for cash. Assets can be classified as illiquid, requiring more time and

complexity to convert into money, or as liquid, allowing for swift conversion into cash. Asset classes—groups of assets with comparable qualities—are used to classify assets in the investment market. Several common asset classifications include the following:

- Stocks

A stock, sometimes referred to as equities or shares, is a single ownership stake in a business or organization. Through stock exchanges, where buyers and sellers can transact in stocks, companies sell their shares to the general public. With the founding of the Amsterdam Stock Exchange in the early 1600s, this type of investing is among the oldest in the world.

A percentage of a company's profits are paid out to investors in the form of dividends on certain stocks, while investors simply purchase and hold onto other stocks in the hopes that their value will increase over time. Despite being a riskier asset class, stocks are widely discussed in the media and are among the most talked-about asset groups.

- Bonds

Investments based on debt are bonds. Essentially, an investor who buys a bond is lending their money to a company or government to support its financial needs. As a bondholder, you get a return on your initial investment in addition to fixed repayments of the money you invested plus interest.

Government bonds and corporate bonds are the two primary categories of bonds. The riskiness of the borrower—that is, the possibility that they won't repay you—is taken into account when rating these bonds. Investment-grade bonds are those with superior ratings, while high-yield bonds are those that are considered riskier. Despite the fact that investment-grade bonds typically provide poor returns, many investors are drawn to them due to their low risk, particularly those who are more risk averse.

- Property

We are all aware with the asset class known as real estate. It includes the residences we occupy, the stores we frequent, and the workplaces we use. A real estate investment is the ownership of both the land and any buildings situated thereon. Despite being seen as a risky investment, real estate is one of the most popular (and costly) asset types in the financial industry. It's well-liked by institutions with multibillion dollar funds that buy and develop real estate only to generate financial returns, in addition to individual investors.

- Goods and Services

Additionally, commodities stand for items that we encounter on a daily basis. A tangible (physical) good that may be exchanged, such raw materials or agricultural goods, is called a commodity. Typical examples include wheat, sugar, oil, and gold. Something must be produced or sold in a comparable quality by numerous individuals or businesses in order to qualify as a commodity. For thousands of years, people have traded and invested in commodities like gold, which are now a common component of many financial portfolios.

- Options

Alternative investments have grown in popularity throughout time, although there used to be very few primary asset classes for investing, such as stocks and bonds. Certain alternatives, such collectibles like wine and art, have been around for a while but weren't as widely available as they are now. Others have emerged as a result of technological advancement. For instance, by making loans available to ordinary investors, fintechs—companies that improve financial services—like Mintos are driving growth in the alternative finance sector. Digital assets such as cryptocurrencies are another example of investments driven by technology.

- Money

Cash is regarded as an asset class even though it's more about saving than investing. The money in your bank account or any savings you may have in a fixed-term deposit are referred to as cash. Since cash is always on hand when investors need it, even in the form of a short-term fixed-term deposit, it is considered a low-risk asset type.

Where should you start if you want to start investing?

There are many different types of investments, and an investor's choice mainly depends on their financial goals and past investing performance. Despite the seemingly endless array of investing alternatives, there is something to fit every taste.

Establishing investing objectives is a terrific place to start. After your budget and goals are somewhat clear, you may start looking into the assets or asset classes that best fit your risk tolerance and financial goals.

An obvious place to start could be with investment platforms that provide basic, automated investing strategies. These methods don't require prior expertise or timely in-depth investigation because they are constructed using expert analysis and data. Exchange-traded funds, which are large investment portfolios in which investors can purchase shares, also offer very simple investment options. They don't need any work on the part of investors because they are managed by investment firms. Alternatively, using investment platforms or brokers, you can conduct your own research and manually make individual investment decisions if you'd prefer more control.

While some investors own a single asset, like a piece of real estate, others have a diverse range of assets, together referred to as an investment portfolio. It's crucial to avoid putting all of your eggs in one basket when building a portfolio. Small amounts of money spread across a variety of assets might be advantageous in order to diversify your investments, which is an investing strategy that balances out higher-risk and lower-risk holdings. By doing this, you can frequently raise your odds of getting the results you anticipated.

Are you prepared to make an investment?
Making your first investment is a significant step. You can use this guide to determine if it's the appropriate move for you.
Many savers are searching for a higher return due to the low interest rates on cash deposits in recent years.

Investing entails assuming financial risks. This isn't always a bad thing—in fact, taking on greater risk may provide higher returns—but you should be ready to lose part or all of your assets if you decide to invest.

It's important to evaluate your finances and make sure you have the required protections in place before making any investments.

You want to invest, but why?
Depending on your financial objectives, you should decide whether to invest or hold cash reserves.

Are you merely trying to increase your wealth? Or are you trying to get a steady job? Is there a certain income you must have, or a certain amount you would like your money to grow by?

Generally speaking, to increase the likelihood that your investments will weather market downturns, you should be willing to part with your funds for a minimum of five years. This is especially crucial if you're almost done working.

Setting objectives will assist you in determining the level of risk you must accept in order to realize your objectives.

The following are some common instances of financial objectives and investment factors:

- Purchasing a home: If you intend to purchase within the next five years, transfer your savings to a lifetime or cash individual savings account. Consider an investing

lifetime Isa to take advantage of government benefits if you have more than five years left on your mortgage and it's your first residence.
- Getting married: Unless you plan to marry in at least five years, cash savings are probably a better option.
- Education costs for a child Putting money into a junior Isa can help you grow it, and the money will have up to eighteen years to weather market downturns.
- Retirement: If you're not going to go over your annual allowance, it can be beneficial to make extra voluntary payments to your pension.

Do you owe money?

Ensure that your debts are managed. Interest payments on your debt will probably be more expensive than the profits you make on assets.

If the interest rates are low, mortgages and other forms of student debt are an exception.

Prior to investing, try to pay off all of your debt or at least reduce it to a manageable amount.

Do you have savings for emergencies?
Do you have any extra cash on hand? You should have some emergency savings before you risk your money.

It is generally advised to save at least three months' worth of expenses before making any investments. Consider your future expenses as well, since you may have to make a loss on your investment withdrawal if you need to take money out of it immediately.

It is unlikely to be beneficial to pause workplace pension contributions in order to invest because you would lose out on tax benefits and employer contributions.

Are you aware of the danger you are assuming?
It's crucial to comprehend the hazards associated with investing and choose your level of risk tolerance.

A high-risk strategy is probably not for you if you don't think you could sleep at night in the event that the markets were volatile, even if you had a lengthy time horizon and plenty of cash on hand.

If you are unaware of the investment you are making, it is impossible to evaluate risk. For example, are you truly aware of the difficulties that commercial real estate faces?

Be truthful, and if in doubt, think about making simpler, more controlled investments like stocks and bonds.

Are there any "risk-free" investments?
Certain investments, like government and corporate bonds, are thought to be less risky than others.

You cannot, however, totally remove the risk. In the case of corporate bonds, for instance, the bond issuer might fail. In this scenario, the bond loses all of its value since it is unable to make interest payments or pay back the loan when it is due.

In actuality, the creditworthiness of the issuer has a major impact on how risky a bond is. Government bonds from nations unlikely to default on interest or capital repayments are viewed as a safer option and would have a higher score, like AAA. This is indicated by a credit rating ranging from C to AAA.

It is nearly always necessary to take on more risk if you want to maximize your potential return. Because of this, it's critical to build a diverse portfolio that includes a range of investments appropriate for your risk tolerance.

Is it wise to purchase cryptocurrency?
You can send money anywhere in the globe using digital currencies like bitcoin, and there are plenty more, without worrying about exchange rates. Instead of a value guarantee from a financial organization like the Bank of England, it is supported by computer code.

In the past, there have been some really painful bitcoin crashes. For instance, there was a significant decline in trust in cryptocurrencies in 2022 as a result of the failure of the trading site FTX.

It can be very dangerous to pursue an investment that can record such large losses in such a short period of time.

Additionally, keep in mind that the Financial Conduct Authority does not oversee cryptocurrencies, meaning you will not have much protection in the event that something goes wrong.

Is it wise to heed financial advice?
Many investors decide for themselves without consulting a broker. However, DIY demands confidence, knowledge, and time.

By seeking financial guidance, you may discuss all of the aforementioned issues and make sure that your assets are precisely matched to your long-term requirements.

How can one begin investing?
If you think you're ready to make an investment, check out our investment guidelines, which explain the various alternatives and how investing operates.

You won't be required to pay taxes on any earnings you make if you invest in an innovative finance Isa, junior Isa, or stocks and shares Isa.

Fund supermarkets, another name for online investing platforms, provide Isas with a simple and affordable means of purchasing and disposing of investments. Look up Which? Here are some suggested providers.

Selecting a platform and tax wrapper is simply the first step. The following are the top five factors to think about when investing:

- How you've been acting A key component of financial success is consistent money addition to your portfolio.
- Allocating assets: You can take on as much risk as you're comfortable with if you find the ideal balance for your investments in bonds, stocks, and other asset classes.
- Charges, expenses, and fees Whether or not your investments increase, fees will still apply, so be sure you're not overpaying.
- Selection of individual investments - Though most people are unwilling to acknowledge it, chance will play a bigger role in your success than the money or shares you purchase.
- Taxes: You can avoid paying too much in dividends or capital gains tax by contributing to an IRA or pension.

Which should you invest: recurring savings or a single sum?

Consistent saving gives you the chance to benefit from market swings. This approach is referred to as "pound cost averaging."

The practice of consistently investing the same amount, typically on a monthly basis, to mitigate the effects of the highs and lows of the price of your selected investment is known as pound cost averaging.

Pound cost averaging has the effect of causing you to regularly purchase assets at varying prices as opposed to purchasing at a single price. Additionally, you can come out ahead financially while riding out market fluctuations compared to making a flat sum investment.

You would still have the same amount of money and shares if you made an investment in one single sum. Even when the share price stays the same as when you first started investing, you can wind up with more shares and, as a result, some capital growth if you make regular investments.

The possible drawback of pound cost averaging over lump sum investing is that you may lose out on some value gain if your investment appreciates over time.

Watch out for investment frauds

An investment scam happens when someone presents you with a phony, yet frequently enticing, chance to earn provided you part with your money.

The offer may appear to be entirely reasonable at first glance. However, you'll typically lose some or all of your money.

Investments involving unregulated products should also be avoided as they are not subject to Financial Conduct Authority (FCA) regulations and carry a significantly higher risk.

Unregulated investments are typically not covered by the Financial Services Compensation Scheme (FSCS) and are not safeguarded in the same manner as regulated savings and investments.

Check the FCA's warning list and see if the company is registered there to see if you are dealing with a recognized scammer.

You should report any investment scams you believe have targeted you to the FCA Scam Smart website.

CHAPTER 8
INVESTMENT ISN'T ONLY FOR RICH PEOPLE

What is the number of times you have told yourself that you want to start investing? But, you never seem to find the time, resources, or self-assurance to begin for whatever reason. Are you afraid to invest in the stock market? If so, simply remember that you're not by yourself. Many people place a higher value on cash than they do on assets, particularly millennials. It is simple to prioritize your immediate demands over your long-term requirements, but regrettably, this way of thinking will not benefit you down the road. You need to quit depending on your savings and checking accounts to help you accumulate wealth if you want to start doing so. They were not designed to make you wealthy, so you must use a different approach in order to achieve something better. In order to create new realities for yourself in 2019, begin investing and give up on outdated beliefs and routines.

You will undoubtedly miss what matters tomorrow if you are only concerned with the here and now. You have to take care of all of your short- and long-term financial demands (not just some) if you want your life to be better later on. It's time to multitask and get out of your own way. Putting money away won't lead to wealth accumulation. You truly lose it as a result of it. If all you do is set aside money and put it in a savings account, the value of that money will keep going down every year. We refer to this as inflation. The purchase value of money is depleted by inflation every year by 2 to 3 percent, so stuffing cash beneath your mattress or in a savings account won't make up for it. Consider how many groceries you could have purchased five years ago for $100, for instance. How many groceries can you buy today with $100? Inflation is the cause of this reduction. Every year, living expenses increase and life becomes more costly. Now is the perfect moment to discover how to make money while you sleep by investing it rather than conserving it if you want to be wealthy.

You have to approach stock market investment with a long-term perspective if you want to start thinking like someone who is generating wealth. It is vital for investors to understand that market declines are inevitable. With the way things are currently going, 2019 might potentially see a significant downturn.

Will you allow that to frighten you? It's better to be informed than afraid at this point. You do realize that life's greatest lessons come from the most trying times? So why not start reading, learning, and accumulating riches right away? The stock market can drop 20–30% in any given year, and this has really happened more than once in the previous 50 years. But if you look past your feelings and consider how long-term wealth development is, you'll realize that the stock market has historically returned between 8 and 10 percent. There are instances when the stock market is down and instances when it is up. There are good games and bad games, just like in basketball. But if you don't participate in the game at all, you will never be the champion.

An essential component of any financial plan is investing. Over time, trading securities such as stocks, exchange-traded funds (ETFs), and others can help you accumulate money. Furthermore, it's usually best to start investing as soon as possible. The good news is that you may get started without needing a sizable sum of extra money. Knowing where to put your money to maximize your returns is the key to making smart investments with little money.

To assist you in achieving your financial objectives, you can also collaborate with a financial advisor who will oversee the complete asset allocation procedure.

What is the best way to begin investing small amounts of money?

The idea that you need to have hundreds or thousands of dollars to enter the market is one common misperception about how to begin investing. Although it is occasionally the case for some assets, including hedge funds, it is more of an anomaly than the norm. What is the required amount of money to begin investing?

To put it briefly, it depends on what kind of investments you wish to make. However, you may start trading stocks, ETFs, and even cryptocurrencies for as little as $100. If you invest less, can it possibly take you longer to accumulate wealth? Maybe. However, if you wait until you have more funds to invest, you may lose out on the compounding effect.

Investing is placing money in the market so that compound interest can expand it. That is an alternative method of putting the interest you receive on your subject. The longer you stay in the market, the longer you can take advantage of compounding. Therefore, investment will still pay off in the long run, even if all you have to spare is $25 or $50 a month.

How to Make Little Investments
The key to investing on a tight budget is understanding how to make every dollar matter. For someone with little funds to invest, there are investing vehicles and platforms that are probably more helpful, at least initially.

Here are a few of the most astute methods of making smaller-scale investments:

Purchasing Partial Stocks
An ownership position in a corporation is represented by a stock share. When trading stock shares, you typically purchase entire shares. Conversely, fractional share trading enables you to invest in businesses little by little.

Fractional share trading is available through several brokerages, and you can start purchasing shares for as low as $1. You can keep making deposits to buy more fractional shares in amounts that suit your spending plan.

You can own shares of more expensive firms and dip your toes in the market by investing in fractional shares. Rather than spending $100 on a single blue-chip stock, for example, you could divide that same cash among fractional shares in ten distinct elite corporations.

Since you can receive a variety of securities in one investing vehicle, purchasing fractional shares of ETFs may be even more advantageous. By spreading your investment across a number of ETFs, you can diversify to reduce risk and get exposure to a variety of sectors and businesses.

Putting Spare Change Into Investment
With spare change investing applications, you may invest with simply your spare change, usually in pre-selected ETFs. These apps often track your spending, round up transactions, and link to your

bank account. After that, the rounded amount is invested on your behalf.

There are benefits to investing with spare change apps since you can start with actual cents. Due to the fact that you often invest in ETFs rather than needing to choose individual equities, these applications can help facilitate diversification.

If spare change applications appeal to you as a low-cost investment alternative, be sure to look into any potential costs. And consider the variety of assets available. Purchasing an ETF using a spare change app that is comparable to one you now purchase fractional shares of through your brokerage, for instance, could cause overlap and weaken your diversification strategy.

Crowdfunded Real Estate and REITs
Due to its low correlation with the stock market and ability to act as a hedge against inflation, real estate can be a wonderful investment. It can be challenging, though, to purchase a rental property or a fix-and-flip property if you lack the thousands of dollars needed for a down payment and house upgrades.

For investors with limited capital, real estate investment trusts (REITs) and crowdfunded real estate provide an entry point. A real estate investment trust (REIT) is a company that holds real estate and distributes dividends to investors. In crowdfunded real estate, you combine your funds with those of other investors in order to receive interest and dividends on your investments.

While some crowdfunding sites and REITs may demand $10,000, $25,000, or more to get started, others have far lower requirements. For example, you may be able to purchase a portion of a property for as little as $250 or $500.

Putting money into crowdfunded homes or Real Estate Investment Trusts (REITs) might help you diversify your portfolio in innovative ways. It's important to keep in mind that these investments typically have lengthier holding periods. Therefore, you could have to wait five years or longer to get your initial investment back, as opposed to having the flexibility to cash out of your investment whenever you wanted to with stocks or ETFs.

Investing in the Workplace

A 401(k) or other comparable retirement plan offered by your employer can be an excellent way to get started with investing. For instance, you can contribute a portion of your income to a 401(k) plan every pay period. You are able to determine how much to invest based on your earnings and spending plan.

Typical 401(k) investment options include mutual funds, exchange-traded funds (ETFs), index funds, and target-date funds. Even if you choose a smaller initial contribution rate, you can still progressively accumulate money even though you probably won't be able to purchase or sell individual equities.

As your income improves, you can gradually increase the amount you defer. For example, if you receive a 2% raise, you can continue to base your budget on your prior paychecks and increase your contribution rate by 2%. Remember that there might be a minimum amount you have to contribute in order to receive the full match if your company offers a matching contribution.

Automated Advisors
If you lack the additional funds to cover adviser costs, you may want to consider using a robo-advisor platform. Robo-advisors use their own proprietary algorithms to build a portfolio for you. The robo-advisor invests the money you deposit into your account, making adjustments as necessary to meet your investment objectives.

Robo-advisors can be a cheap alternative to traditional financial advisor costs when it comes to investing. And if you schedule regular deposits into your account, you can use modest sums of money to build wealth on autopilot.

Inter-Peer Financing
Peer-to-peer, or P2P, lending is a kind of crowdfunding where a group of investors pool their resources to support an individual's loan request. The investors receive their money back along with interest.

Peer-to-peer lending is still a viable option for small-scale investors looking to generate substantial returns on their investments, notwithstanding the risk associated with probable borrower default. A few hundred dollars can be invested in one loan, or it might be divided up to fund several loans.

When it comes to P2P lending, it's generally a good idea to assume that risk increases with predicted rate of return. To reduce risk, it could be a good idea to distribute your investing funds among a variety of loans.

If you're prepared to enter the market but haven't yet risen to the top of the financial elite, it's important to understand how to invest with modest funds. Utilizing the various avenues available to you for making tiny investments can assist you in building a well-rounded portfolio that suits your requirements, objectives, and risk tolerance.

Here are three strategies to get you started in the investment game:
1. Give up the notion that only wealthy people invest.

You have the capacity to build an affluent family even though you may not come from one. You have the ability to shape your own reality, so if accumulating riches is important to you, begin adopting the lifestyle of the affluent. You've somehow convinced yourself of a lie that prevents you from making investments. You believe it to be difficult and overly complicated for you. But you can start writing a new story, exactly as you wrote the previous one. Get started learning more about investing; as you gain knowledge, your confidence will increase. Being wealthy, you possess all the necessary resources to begin transforming this concept into a material reality.

2. Decide on a monthly investment amount.

For some reason, a lot of people think that investing millions of dollars is necessary. As a result, if we don't have much money to invest, we don't invest at all. We can also modify the tale of this as well. The stock values of some of the most well-known household brand names are less than $300. View a list of every company that is included in the S&P 500. Look up the stock values of the names of companies you are familiar with. Check to see whether you would feel comfortable investing in any inexpensive stocks. You'll be shocked to learn how many businesses are within the reach of first-time investors. By purchasing stock in a company, you too can become a part owner as long as you are willing and able.

3. Create a trading account

A checking account, savings account, and brokerage account are the three primary types of accounts that each individual ought to possess. Three important characteristics are what you should search for in a superb brokerage account: 1) No minimum amount required, 2) Transaction/broker fees are minimal (less than $10), and 3) the interface and educational materials are simple. Consider opening a brokerage account with no minimum if you don't have a lot of money to begin with.

You are on the wrong track if your monthly income is sufficient to spend on someone else or a business, but not enough to save for your personal needs. To secure your financial future, you must begin investing with the same drive that you use to earn money. Small sums of money should be invested in your brokerage account until it becomes second nature to you. Your life will begin to change before your very eyes if you adopt the routines and mindset of an investor.

CHAPTER 9
SAVE WHILE SLEEPING

There may seem to be never enough hours in a day to do everything you want to get done. Work, relationships, fitness—the list is endless. But there is good news when it comes to earning money. Saving and investing are two easy and uncomplicated ways to earn money even while you sleep.

You're not alone if you've been feeling like you should start saving for retirement but don't know where to begin. According to an Ontario Securities Commission report from 2017, 80% of millennials in Canada save money, but only approximately half invest.

Seven out of ten respondents stated in the research that they are unable to invest because of other financial priorities. Approximately 60% of those surveyed stated that they were either afraid of losing money or didn't know enough about investing.

These results are not unexpected. Anything new might be frightening to start. However, long-term investing is not as hard as it might seem. You can even earn money while you sleep, in fact. This isn't real if it sounds too good to be true! It's crucial to stress that long-term investing won't make you wealthy right away.

Listed below are a few strategies for investing your money to grow at a risk you can handle.

1. Interest compounded

It is advisable to begin investing and saving as soon as feasible. This allows you to benefit from compound interest's magic and can help you with your "how to make money" conundrum.

You can earn interest on your money in a number of ways. Establishing a savings account at a bank is the easiest. These accounts are almost risk-free, but their interest rates are typically lower than what you could get by investing in other assets. Another lower-risk investment with a fixed interest rate is guaranteed income certificates. Another option is to purchase business or government bonds. You receive interest from the organization to which you lend or deposit money in exchange for the right to keep your cash on hand. The wonderful aspect is that this interest compounds.

Investing in bonds can be done easily via exchange-traded funds, or ETFs. You may eliminate a large portion of the possible risk associated with purchasing a bond from a single firm by combining multiple bonds into one investment, such as an ETF. Equities are another asset class that ETFs can track and often yield larger returns.

Let's go back to the bit about compounding. This implies that you receive interest on both your initial investment and your interest. Calculating compound interest demonstrates how this operates. For instance, after ten years, you would have more than $1,200 if you invested $1,000 in an investment with a 2% annual interest rate. That's more than $200 you made doing nothing at all. Yes, it isn't much. However, what if you made a commitment to set aside $50 every month for that time? You would have $7,850 after ten years, with interest earnings of more than $850. This is where the concept of making money while you sleep originated.

2. Payouts

Companies that distribute a portion of their profits to their shareholders are those that have dividend-paying stocks. You obtain a dividend if you purchase stock in such a business. For instance, if you buy $1,000 worth of the company's shares and it pays a 0.5% annual dividend, you will receive $5 annually. Once more, while that might not seem like much, it builds up over time and with larger sums of money. A lot of well-known investors strongly support dividends. Once more, owning the stock is all that is required of you in order to effectively make money. Do you see a trend here?

It is significant to remember that corporations have the option to increase or decrease their dividend payments.

3. Put dividends back into your account!
The ability to reinvest earnings as soon as you receive them is another wonderful feature of dividends. We witness the force of compounding in action once more. You add your dividend income to your initial investment rather than wasting it. Your money will rise faster as a result. You thus receive higher returns and potential dividend payments. A lot of investment funds automatically reinvest your dividends.

4. Additional sources of income (but while you're awake)

There are different methods to create money while going about your everyday activities, even though long-term investing is a fantastic technique to do it while you sleep. Consider cash-back initiatives. These schemes, which are frequently provided by banks and credit card issuers, reimburse you in cash for a predetermined portion of the total amount you spend on your credit or debit card. With a 1% cashback credit card, for instance, you can receive $10 for each $1,000 you spend. This adds up, particularly if you were going to spend the money otherwise.

Numerous customer reward programs are available to you that let you make money both directly and indirectly. Some provide you with savings on further purchases, such as reward points that may be redeemed for airfare or lodging discounts at certain hotel or airline companies.

Take it gradually at first and ask for assistance if necessary.

Recall that you don't require a large sum of money to begin investing. $100 or even $50 every month might have a significant impact. It also doesn't take a lot of effort. You can look at a few possibilities for purchasing Fidelity ETFs to get started. The most important thing is to begin. Without saving, money cannot increase.

The ability to generate income while they sleep is a trait shared by prosperous businesspeople. They are experts at generating passive income and most likely have multiple sources of it flowing in.

The idea of earning money while you sleep could seem unreachable if you're finding it difficult to manage even one active source of income.

I will not be dishonest. It might require some effort. But anyone can become financially independent with passive income.

How can one obtain passive income?
People refer to passive income when they discuss earning money while you sleep. It is money that you receive without having to put in any effort to earn it. It requires your input to start moving, but once it does, it can move forward with little assistance.

Like the majority of individuals, you are not currently receiving passive money from your employment. You are exchanging money for time.

Because time is restricted when you exclusively work that way, you ultimately cap your earning potential. Hours in a day, days in a week, weeks in a month, and so on are limited.

"If you don't find a way to make money while you sleep, you will work until you die," as Warren Buffet said it best.

Though it's a harsh reality, that's the reason you're reading this post at this very moment.

Let's be clear before we continue: every passive income source demands an initial investment.

There are two ways that you can invest that money:
- Financial
- Effort

Before you get any benefits, you have to do one of those things.

Recall that you should not put your trust in anyone attempting to sell you a miracle medication. They are not real. To be paid, you must work, but if you put in the correct effort, you can make money while you sleep.

How to Generate Recurring Income
By now, you probably have a general idea of it. You already know that it's time to work less, not more.
Now that you're ready... Genuine, authentic, trustworthy, ethical, and healthful methods to earn money while you sleep.

1. Make Stock Market investments
Since it's arguably the most evident passive income source, I'll start with it. The initial investment in investing requires funds, which can be obtained through a conventional brokerage such as Fidelity or Charles Schwab.

If you think you don't have enough money to start, there are a ton of micro-investing apps available today that take that obstacle away.

Although microinvesting only yields marginal returns, it is a method by which novice investors can begin generating modest sums of passive income. You'll need to start making bigger investments if you want to increase that income.

2. Let a Room Become Rental
If you feel like you don't have a lot of time or money to invest in other ideas, this is an excellent place to start even if it may not be the most glamorous way to make money while you sleep.

One of the greatest ways to rent a room—or your entire house—to guests from out of town is through Airbnb. Living in a major city or popular tourist spot increases your earning possibilities. This might be a good strategy to help defray the cost of your mortgage payments in addition to providing passive income.

3. Create a Blog to Get Paid by Affiliates
Prominent bloggers—those with six-figure income reports, for example—make blogging appear quite simple. They write, publish content on social media, take pictures, and lead idyllic lives while traveling over Europe in a boat or on a rucksack.

These are actual people that have worked really hard to reach their current position.

Not every blogger will reach that level. The great majority won't even make six figures every month, in actuality.

That is partially due to their leaving just before things start to take up. The fact that not everyone can profit significantly from a blog is the second factor. similar to how not every coffee shop will grow into a large conglomerate like Starbucks.

However, the typical blogger can generate passive income from their site by investing time and effort into its growth.

There are a few more ways for bloggers to do this, but most people immediately think of affiliate marketing.

AFFILIATE MARKETING: WHAT IS IT?
This is only one of several strategies for making money off of blogs. It occurs when you include a unique link promoting a certain brand or business in your blog entries. You then be paid a little amount of

money (also known as affiliate income) when one of your readers clicks on that link and purchases something.

People can still click on those links and generate revenue for you even weeks, months, or even years after you publish those articles. That's the point where you can earn money while you sleep.

You'll need to put a lot of time and effort into your site before you can start making money with affiliate marketing. Before you may use affiliate networks, you must reach a particular level of audience and page view growth.

There isn't just one target number. Your blog will determine a lot of this.

It's true that some bloggers who receive large affiliate incomes don't have a ton of page views.

Our wonderful friend Michelle Schroeder-Gardner at Making Sense of Cents is a prime example. She teaches other bloggers her exact method in her course Making Sense of Affiliate Marketing. She consistently makes about $50,000 a month from affiliate marketing.

4. Develop a Sellable Product

Making your own product is another fantastic option to make money while you sleep if you have a blog. The time needed to develop and market the product is the first investment. In order for your audience to believe they will receive value for their money, you must also earn their trust.

Through their blogs, bloggers can offer a wide range of products, including:

- Printable
- Merchandise
- E-books
- Courses (more on this in the point that follows)

Our pals Julie and Cody from Gold City Ventures are amazing side giggers who sell printables on Etsy! They've been so successful that they went so far as to develop a course where they share their greatest hustle secrets on Etsy.

Maintaining your website once you've developed your product and begun promoting it calls for some routine maintenance.

Marketing any kind of product requires having an email list. This will keep turning site visitors into paying clients in a passive manner.

Being in total control of your product, from production to marketing to sales, is one of the best things about selling your own goods. Here, you are the one in control.

5. Establish an Online Program

One approach to impart useful knowledge to others is through the sale of online courses. You should be an expert in the subject matter of your course, and you should be confident that others will find it useful.

For this reason, the Facebook Side Hustle course was developed by Laptop Empires creators Mike Yanda and Bobby Hoyt. These two are essentially Facebook ad experts; they've made good money from running them and discovered that others may start this lucrative side business by taking a course.

Creating a course requires a significant effort investment. Selling courses is a profitable approach to interact with your audience and provide them with some real-world assistance.

6. Property

Real estate investing is probably going to remain a reliable source of passive income for a long time. This is because the land is limited, much like time. Everybody needs a place to live, businesses need a place to open for business, and so forth.

Here are three real estate-based strategies to earn money while you slumber:

- Properties for rent. This can be either residential or commercial and can boost your monthly cash flow through rental income.
- Adjust and rotate. In this scenario, you buy houses that require renovation, patch them up, and resell them for a bigger sum of money.
- REITs. Real Estate Investment Trust is what it stands for. It's commercial real estate investing for regular people, not for

millionaires. It's highly recommended to check out Fundrise.

7. Direct Delivery

The greatest number of individuals to date, 2.14 billion, is predicted to buy online in 2021.

For this reason, using a platform like Shopify to launch your own online store might enable you to generate passive revenue.

When using drop shipping, you should first:
- Create a website (you can use Shopify for this).
- Include products from certain manufacturers on your website.
- That good ships from the manufacturer, not you, when someone buys it.
- Spend money for the goods, yet make more money than what is sold.

Drop shipping is distinct in that it eliminates the need for inventory sourcing and storage. You merely create and oversee the website.

You can start making money while you sleep by selling things if your website is correctly designed and promoted.

8. Launch a Channel on YouTube

Similar to bloggers, not every YouTuber will become wealthy. That's simply the way things are. Still, YouTube is a great place to share tales, do do-it-yourself projects, provide guides, and more.

On YouTube, you can make money from
- Ad revenue. Your videos' links direct visitors to buyable goods and services.
- Endorsements. While it's not totally passive, you can be compensated for endorsing goods and businesses that you think are good.
- Making things on your own. This might be merchandise, online courses you offer, etc.

9. Market Stock Images

Photographers of all skill levels can sell their images to stock photo marketplaces such as Shutterstock, SmugMug, iStock, and others.

You can profit anywhere from 20% to 60% of the price of material downloads, depending on the website.

10. Compose an electronic book

Inexperienced authors can write and sell ebooks to generate passive money using Amazon Kindle

Direct Publishing. It goes without saying that this requires an investment: writing a book!

Self-publishing gives you total control over your book. But it's not as easy as it looks. It involves understanding how to market your work, as well as what kinds of things consumers are interested in reading.

Thankfully, there are many of people providing excellent, practical guidance on where to begin.

11. Make sales on Amazon FBA

The acronym for Fulfillment by Amazon is FBA. Through this service, individual sellers can discover things they want to sell, have them sent to Amazon, and let Amazon handle the product's sale and delivery to customers.

Among the many products you can sell with Amazon FBA are
- Books.
- Shop arbitrage
- items in bulk
- DVDs

My cousin made over $25,000 in their first year of selling secondhand books through Amazon FBA, and they recently resigned their day job as a registered CPA. This was accomplished by spending only a few hours every week sourcing books (Amazon offers a tool that makes this process simple).

You can see how passive it is when you take into account that Amazon manages customer service, payments, delivery, and sales.

12. Purchase an Already-Found Website

You probably already know that creating a blog requires a lot of time and effort from what you've read previously. It may take several months for your website to turn a profit. Some speed up this procedure by paying upwards of $1,000+ for pre-existing websites.

Flippa offers pre-existing blogs and websites for sale, providing you with details such as:
- Name and URL of the website
- Site's age
- What kind of webpage
- Net profit each month

As with any financial commitment, you should thoroughly investigate each site before moving further.

13. Get a Music License

Similar to the sale of stock pictures, you can earn passive money by selling your own original music. You get paid when someone purchases your music to use in YouTube videos, video games, advertisements, and other media. The websites that sell your music do charge a commission.

These well-known websites are great for selling your music:
- LuckStock
- Soundotcom
- AudioJungle
- PremiumBeat

14. Create and Market Personalized Items

Artists seeking a way to monetize their creations can create images for sale on t-shirts, posters, coffee mugs, hats, phone covers, and other items.

The following websites can produce and market the products for you when you finish the design process. Print-on-demand is the term used to describe this, and you can read more about it on a number of websites.

Among the websites are:
- Threadless
- CafePress
- TeeSpring

15. Promote an App

Another way to earn money while you sleep is to create and sell an app if you know how to code. When the software is sold, you receive passive revenue in exchange for the time and skills you invested in its creation.

Over time, even the sales of mobile apps advertised for a few dollars can mount up.

16. Establish a Community of Members

The ability to interact with people worldwide is one of the best things about working from home, and it's ideal for building a membership community.

On a membership site, users can pay to interact with other members of your club or access special information via your website or social media group.

If you already have a website, you may create and manage memberships with a plugin like Membermouse. You receive the full sign-up cost each time a new member joins, including with renewals.

Recurring payments can be scheduled at any time you like, and most members will continue to pay as long as they believe your offerings are worthwhile.

Providing each member with a useful service and updating information frequently are essential components of a successful membership community.

17. Podbean

Since you do need to be awake during the podcast recording process, it is technically not called passive. But, after you've begun expanding your listenership, you can incorporate more sources of income into your podcast.

This may develop become the podcasting industry's passive revenue stream.

Podcasters can profit from affiliate marketing just like bloggers can. You can post product links in newsletters, on your website, or on social media as you begin to increase your subscriber base.

Additionally, there are chances to sell products bearing your podcast's logo prominently displayed or sponsored content via a podcast. With membership communities, you can charge subscribers extra for access to unique content, making it a simple method to integrate with podcasts.

18. Hire a Car

Although everyone has heard of rideshare drivers, did you realize that there are services that allow people to rent their cars when they're not using them?

Consider renting out your car if you have one that you don't need every day in order to make some extra cash. It's the perfect time to join a carsharing club because of the current rental car scarcity that is affecting the United States.

This service is provided by multiple businesses, including:
- Turo
- Use Vehicle Sharing
- Escape
- Zipcar

Even if some of these carsharing programs are only available in large cities or close to airports, it's still worthwhile to give them a shot if you have a car that you don't use often or can use while you're on vacation or out of town.

19. Use a High-Yield Savings Account to Conserve Money

The average payout on a bank's regular savings account is a pitiful 0.01%. Although having funds placed aside in a designated account is a terrific idea, regular accounts are not the only options.

If you're looking to park some money, consider certificates of deposit or high-yield savings accounts.

Even if they're not making as much money as they used to, high-yield savings accounts still provide greater interest rates than conventional savings accounts.

Make sure you are aware of the minimum deposit amount and the period of time your money must stay in the account before selecting this option.

Thankfully, there are other high-yield account options available online, such as Marcus, American Express, Synchrony and plenty others

Additionally, you might look into opportunities at the credit union or bank in your area.

20. Loans from Peers to Peers

Lending money to borrowers who might not be able to get it through conventional lending channels is known as peer-to-peer, or P2P, lending.

It was once challenging to assess the risk and expected growth of each individual if you were interested in investing in P2P lending. But now that technology has advanced, you may find websites that handle this meticulous labor for you.

You can lend capital (money) to people who are borrowing for particular industries, like real estate, using websites like PeerStreet. If your investment is successful, you get paid interest each month. You just need to decide how much to invest and where to put it.

www.ingramcontent.com/pod-product-compliance
Lightning Source LLC
Chambersburg PA
CBHW071208240526
45470CB00018B/1636